Last Entry Point

Last Entry Point

Stories of Danger and Death
in the Boundary Waters

JOE FRIEDRICHS

MINNESOTA
HISTORICAL
SOCIETY PRESS

Portions of this book, in different forms, were previously published
in the *Star Tribune*, on KFAI Radio, on WTIP Radio, and in
Northern Wilds magazine.

Maps by Cat Saari, based on OpenStreetMap. OpenStreetMap is
open data, licensed under the Open Data Commons Open
Database License (opendatacommons.org/licenses/odbl) by
the OpenStreetMap Foundation (osmfoundation.org). See
openstreetmap.org/copyright.

mnhspress.org

The Minnesota Historical Society Press is a member of the
Association of University Presses.

Manufactured in the United States of America

10 9 8 7 6 5 4 3 2 1

♾ The paper used in this publication meets the minimum
requirements of the American National Standard for Information
Sciences—Permanence for Printed Library Materials,
ANSI Z39.48–1984.

International Standard Book Number
ISBN: 978-1-68134-286-3 (paper)
ISBN: 978-1-68134-287-0 (e-book)

Library of Congress Control Number: 2023950362

For
Carley

Contents

Map of locations mentioned in this book

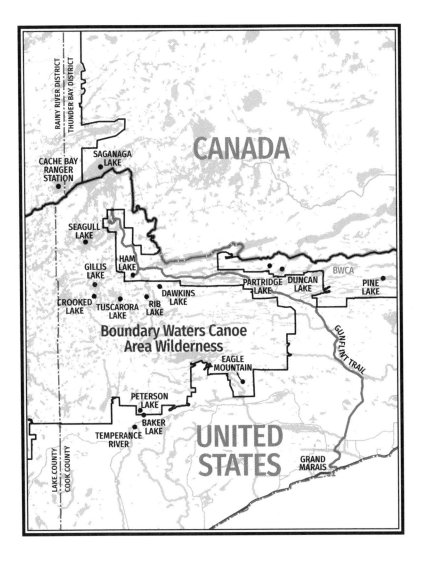

Introduction

The death notices are always short. They come in the form of a press release: usually nothing more than a couple of paragraphs, often with a quote from the local sheriff. Other than that, details are scant after someone dies in the Boundary Waters.

The Boundary Waters Canoe Area Wilderness (BWCA) encompasses more than a million acres of pristine and remote boreal forest in the far reaches of northeastern Minnesota. The US Forest Service manages the landscape. Across the BWCA and adjacent Quetico Provincial Park in Canada, motors of any kind, for the most part, are not allowed. It is largely a quiet space, inhabited by moose, wolves, bears, and other species that tend to captivate the human spirit. These wild creatures roam through a collection of dense forests, deep lakes, and thousands of flowing waterways. It is a setting of natural balance, often romanticized by visions of white pines, singing loons, and breathtaking sunsets. It is also a harsh landscape. Winter temperatures often dip to thirty below zero or colder. With such brutal cold, it's not uncommon for the thousand-plus lakes inside the wilderness area to be covered in ice for more than half the year. When the waters do open, relentless summer winds, massive wildfires, and all manner of insects and wild creatures can make life challenging for human visitors.

As a journalist who lives near the Boundary Waters, I find out when people die in this remote pocket of the globe. The information typically arrives from law enforcement located near Duluth, Ely, or Grand Marais. News reporters have to pry if they want more information.

On May 20, 2020, the Cook County Sheriff's Department in Grand Marais, Minnesota, sent a press release to media outlets across the state. It read, in part: "The Cook County Sheriff's Office 911 Dispatch was notified of an overturned canoe on Tuscarora Lake at approximately 1:51 p.m., today. It was learned that three people were in a canoe which had capsized on Tuscarora Lake. Two of the people swam to an island and one, a 29-year-old male, was reported missing. Identity is being withheld pending notification of family. No further information at this time."

Just the facts. Bare bones, at that. It turns out the twenty-nine-year-old male was Billy Cameron from Indiana. His death is the genesis of this book.

I've been a news reporter on the edge of the Boundary Waters since 2014. In the decade following the start of my tenure here, more than a dozen people have died in this, the most-visited wilderness area in the nation. During a summer thunderstorm in 2016, a tree fell on Minnesota governor Tim Walz's brother on Duncan Lake, killing him. There have been numerous drownings. Wayne Morrow, Michael Hickey, Lester Hochstetler, and Joseph Fedick—they all died in the water here. Search and rescue found a Texas man, Mike Brown, floating dead on Seagull Lake in 2023. He was wearing a life jacket. Each death meant another press release. The notifications continually told little of what happened. Anecdotes were completely absent.

It was Cameron's story that broke me. After reading his death notice on air at WTIP, the community radio station in Grand Marais, our news department posted a short, two-hundred-word story online. This was during the early days of the COVID-19 pandemic, May 2020. A young man died on a lake in the Boundary Waters. The story could have ended there. Instead, I found Cameron's profile on Facebook. His girlfriend, Nataly Yokhanis, posted something on his wall about the situation. I contacted Yokhanis and asked if she wanted to talk about Cameron and what had happened to him. She did.

Prior to recording an interview, we laid down some ground rules. The idea in talking about Cameron's death was to educate people, not scare them. Yokhanis, who is featured in this book, wanted to immediately use Cameron's death as a cautionary tale. "That water is cold," she wanted people to know. Others who planned to paddle in this wilderness, not just in May 2020 but every spring and early summer from that moment on, needed to know how serious it is to fall from a canoe into a Boundary Waters lake. Cameron's accidental death might save the lives of other canoeists, Yokhanis told me. The interview hit the airwaves. Of those listeners who shared their reactions with me, most felt sorrow and sympathy for Yokhanis. Others were horrified. But some were angry. It was not fair to request an interview from someone in a moment of immense pain and suffering, they said. They wanted the story, and the people involved, to be left alone. Talking about death, it turns out, is terrifying for some people.

In this book, you're going to read about people who lost their lives in the Boundary Waters. Yes, people die here. Better a cruel truth than a comfortable delusion, as Edward Abbey said. The acclaimed environmental writer also said, "You can't study the darkness by flooding it with light." Some of the stories shared in this book are disturbing and packed with emotion, as situations involving unexpected death typically are. Just like with the Yokhanis interview, the purpose of sharing these stories is to educate, not to scare. Better planning. Utilizing situational awareness. Waiting. These simple steps could have prevented many of the deaths you will read about.

At the same time, accidents happen. Nobody expects a towering white pine to fall on their tent while they're sleeping. It happens here. So does lightning. Tornadoes. Hypothermia. The other side of the coin is unnecessary risk, like the behavior of twenty-nine-year-old Chase Winkey when he chose to go cliff jumping into the water of Makwa Lake in 2013. Winkey jumped from a sixty-foot cliff and never surfaced. Authorities found him dead in twenty feet of water the next morning. Outfitters, whether located near Highway 61, at the end of the Gunflint Trail, or in downtown Ely, told me time and again how important it is for people to understand these woods and water aren't here to provide them with entertainment. The Boundary Waters is not an amusement park. In fact, it's not a park at all. It's a federally designated wilderness.

The intention of sharing these sometimes-troubling experiences is to prevent similar accidents, including deaths, from happening here. Stories of people dying can have value, in the way a tree, once cut down, can be made into a table or a bench. It is no longer alive, but it continues to have a purpose. And perhaps above everything else, these stories are here to help us remember what the Boundary Waters is capable of.

PART I

Water and Lightning

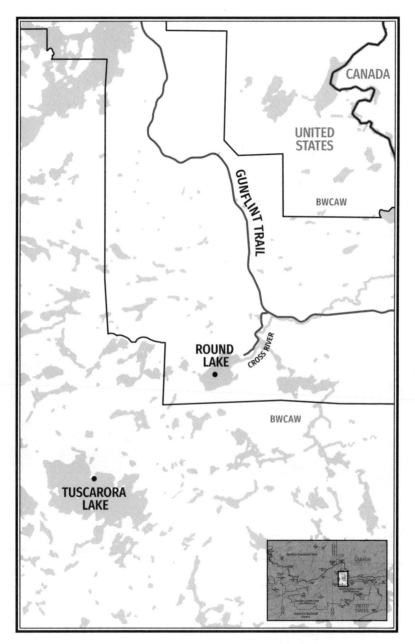

Billy Cameron drowned in Tuscarora Lake.

I

On paper, Billy Cameron did everything right. And he still died in the Boundary Waters.

Cameron and two friends, Curtis Weeks and Taylor Johnson, capsized their canoe on Tuscarora Lake in the BWCA on May 20, 2020. After tumbling from the canoe, Cameron drowned in the frigid waters of Tuscarora Lake, about fifty miles up the Gunflint Trail. The lake is found several portages and lakes in from a popular entry point on Round Lake. Cameron was wearing his life jacket at the time of his death. After entering the water, Cameron and the others tried to get to shore without panicking. Weeks and Johnson made it. Cameron did not. A coroner's report said he died from hypothermia and drowning. He was twenty-nine.

May 2020 was a strange time to be alive. It was the first peak of the COVID-19 pandemic. The world was full of uncertainty. Fear gripped the nation. Five days after Cameron died in the Boundary Waters, George Floyd was murdered on the streets of Minneapolis by a police officer. It was a period of great unrest everywhere you looked.

Few people felt the collective chaos more intensely than Nataly Yokhanis.

"This has broken me at my deepest. I am shattered," Yokhanis, Cameron's girlfriend for many years, told me just days after his death. "I don't think I'll ever be whole again."

Years removed from the onset of a global pandemic, most of society has learned to live with the realities of COVID-19. Similar to the pandemic, Floyd's murder on Chicago Avenue and the subsequent conviction of former Minneapolis police officer Derek Chauvin deeply impacted societies across the globe. As Yokhanis engages with the world and watches the collective human race move forward from these situations, she told me in July 2022 that it's Cameron's drowning that continues to make her feel incomplete. "I have accepted what happened, but nothing will ever be the same," she said.

Yokhanis, a health care professional in Dayton, Ohio, started dating Cameron in July 2011. She was not the spirited outdoorsperson he was, though Cameron's passion for the wilderness was contagious. "He lived for these types of adventures," she said. "Going to the Boundary Waters was something he would talk about all year, staring at maps and calling his friends to talk about the routes. He loved that stuff. He could talk to me about it for hours, and I loved to listen because he was just so excited about going there time and time again."

Cameron, of Noblesville, Indiana, was an avid outdoorsman. He enjoyed visiting Minnesota's north woods and border lakes, and he did so as often as he could. "He knew what he was doing up there," Yokhanis said.

Built like a collegiate athlete, Cameron kept his hair short and his muscles toned. His mother was from Japan. His father was a hardworking white man from the Midwest. The combination of his parents' backgrounds gave Cameron the look of a model, Yokhanis said. "He was beautiful," she told me.

As he moved deeper into his twenties, Cameron made planning a canoe trip to the Boundary Waters a summer tradition. During the 2020 trip, he traveled with Weeks and Johnson to spend time on Tuscarora Lake. With more than thirteen miles of shoreline and ten campsites spread across eight hundred acres, Tuscarora is a popular destination throughout the year. It holds lake trout that grow large in its deep waters, which bottom out at 130 feet.

Tuscarora was familiar territory for the trio from Indiana, and the trip was Cameron's third to the BWCA in recent years. An island campsite in the middle of the lake was Cameron's favorite. It's where the group set up their base of operations this time too, said Yokhanis, who recounted details of the trip from conversations with Weeks and Johnson. Cameron's paddling partners are still largely unable to speak with anyone publicly about the experience and the day their friend Billy died. They have refused all requests from media in Minnesota and beyond to discuss what happened. As painful as the memory is, the authorities, canoe outfitters, and others familiar with the situation all agree the accident that claimed Cameron's life was nobody's fault. "This is a terrible situation, but these things can, and do happen," said Andy McDonnell, co-owner of Tuscarora Lodge and Canoe Outfitters on the Gunflint Trail. "May can be a dangerous time up here. Cold-water drownings are almost like a thing waiting to happen on certain years."

The day Cameron died was unpleasantly windy. It was cold the previous night, with temps dipping to the mid-thirties. This scenario is not unusual in the Boundary Waters, and most who travel in canoe country in late spring do so because many of the pesky insects known to haunt this vast wilderness are not yet in full force. Bugs or no bugs, the temperature slowly warmed up throughout the day in coordination with strong gusts of wind from the south and east. Though it was the third week of the month, the ice had only recently come off some of the larger lakes in the BWCA and along the Gunflint Trail. It's typical for a lake the size of Tuscarora to maintain a surface temperature of about forty-seven degrees in mid-May.

In the early-evening hours, Cameron, who had just celebrated his twenty-ninth birthday the day before, was fishing from shore when his line tangled in the rocky depths. The group had rented a three-person Kevlar canoe known as a Minnesota 3 from nearby Tuscarora Lodge and Canoe Outfitters. Cameron didn't want to snap his line to free the snag, so he and his friends put on their life jackets and hopped in the canoe. After untangling the line, they decided to continue fishing from the canoe near the island. Moments later, they were hit by an easterly gust, and the canoe capsized. The three young men spent nearly fifteen minutes trying to right the watercraft, to no avail. Cameron, the leader and most experienced of the group, decided they should swim toward land.

The men were in peril. Weeks and Johnson were able to reach solid ground safely, though not easily in their heavy boots and clothing. Weeks made it back to the island, haggard and freezing after barreling through waves across a distance greater than the length of a football field. Meanwhile, Johnson ended up on the north shore of the lake after he realized he couldn't move through the waves, but only with them. After reaching land, both Johnson and Weeks started to holler. They could barely hear each other through the wind. At the very least they knew each survived the ordeal. Meanwhile, Cameron was neither heard nor seen. That scene is an image that haunts Yokhanis to this day: Cameron drifting alone in the cold water, fighting for air. His lungs likely filled with water at some point, the result of his desperate gasps for oxygen. The cold water gave him little hope as the situation deteriorated from scary to desperate within minutes, perhaps seconds. Cameron's death was quick. It was not messy.

⌒⌒⌒

Ben Aldritt of Minneapolis expected to travel many miles each day during his group's canoe trip that May. He planned to visit nearly a dozen lakes, starting and ending at Round Lake and Tuscarora Lodge and Canoe Outfitters.

"I love the pre-trip planning and thinking about what campsite we'll get," said Aldritt.

No amount of planning could prepare Aldritt and his companions, Tony Porter and Dan Fuller, for what they would find in the BWCA on the first morning of their trip. After starting early from Round Lake, the crew completed the one-and-a-third-mile portage from Missing Link Lake into Tuscarora with relative ease. The winds from the day before still blew, and the sun was out. About ten minutes after reaching the lake, as they paddled its south shore, they heard shouts in their direction. It was Weeks. As they neared the island campsite, Aldritt could tell the person in distress was waving an object. It was a large stick with a white T-shirt tied to the end. This was an emergency.

After assisting Weeks on the island and confirming he was not injured, the group paddled to the distant shoreline and retrieved Johnson, then brought him back to the island. Cameron still was missing.

"They kept telling us that if anyone could survive this it was Billy," said Aldritt. "They were convinced he was hiking out to get help or that he was just out there in the woods somewhere."

Hours later, after Aldritt and his friends were able to use the satellite phone of another canoe-camper on nearby Missing Link Lake, a search and rescue team was alerted. A floatplane arrived just after 1 PM in search of Cameron. The group's canoe was lost too. The pilot spotted Cameron and the canoe floating in a remote bay in the northwest corner of the lake. Cameron was dead when the pilot pulled him into the plane.

Kylan Hill, a conservation officer for the Minnesota Department of Natural Resources based near Grand Marais, does routine patrols in the BWCA throughout the year. He sounded a note of caution for visitors. Hill said while the air temperature may be comfortable and relatively warm in spring, the water temperature hasn't had time to acclimate.

"It's possible that the water temperature is ten, twenty, or even thirty degrees colder than the air temperature," Hill said.

Aldritt additionally points out that people who come to the BWCA in the early or late seasons need to be prepared for a different type of canoe trip. Absent are afternoon swim sessions or the luxury of wearing sandals across dry portages. Mud, cold, and wind are often reliable realities for BWCA adventures, particularly in May.

"It can get busy around Memorial Day weekend," Aldritt said, "so a lot of us try to get in there before that start of the peak season."

Aldritt, who wears glasses and is a self-described "fishing junkie," will forever recognize the similarities between his group and that of Cameron and his friends. All were experienced canoeists, relatively young, and full of passion for the wilderness. He referenced a Neil Young lyric to sum up their shared spirit for outdoor recreation: "The same thing that makes you live can kill you in the end."

It's believed Cameron went into shock and was unable to breathe—a state called "dry drowning." This is a reality Yokhanis has had to live with since Cameron's mother called her in May 2020 to deliver the tragic news.

"She told me Billy was dead, and my world came crashing down around me," Yokhanis said.

Yokhanis, who was born on a crisp autumn afternoon in 1990, has long, straight black hair. She and Cameron met when they were in their early twenties. Cameron always kept his brown hair cut short "because it was easier to deal with," according to Yokhanis. They were similar in many ways, including possessing a free spirit that wants to learn from different cultures and see firsthand how they function across the planet. Both had an appetite for history, along with shared values to have meaningful relationships with their parents. To celebrate her birthday each year, Cameron would make a point of pausing to reflect on the many amazing things Yokhanis had done over the previous 365 days. "He would sit there and almost go through the year day by day. It was so funny. So sweet," she said.

More recently, for Yokhanis, pausing only brings pain. So she keeps going forward, knowing that a flood of emotion is always looming. "I have bad days," she said.

In a discovery that brought equal parts joy and sadness, Yokhanis learned that Cameron, whom she dated for nearly nine years, had bought a ring and planned to propose when the time was right. While navigating the complex grieving process, Yokhanis wanted to put some action behind the feelings. In a tribute to Cameron, she got a tattoo of a mountain lion that covers most of the upper half of her left leg. Cameron was intrigued by the giant cats and their quest for solitude.

"Billy used to tell me if he ever got a tattoo, he'd get a mountain lion," Yokhanis said.

If there is any reason to find hope in Cameron's death, she said, it's knowing that he lived a good life and that his death will serve as a reminder about keeping safety at the forefront of any trip to the BWCA.

"Safety first, safety second, and maybe coolness third," Yokhanis said. "Accidents are real. That water is cold. Think ahead about if something happens what you are going to do. I can't stress enough to everyone to be as safe as they can."

Among the most difficult aspects of Cameron's death in the Boundary Waters is that it appears he and his friends did keep safety at the forefront of their trip. They were wearing their life jackets and did not panic when they hit the water. They were not attempting to cross an open section of Tuscarora just to keep their trip moving forward on a windy day. There was nothing heroic in attempting to unsnag Cameron's fishing line from the bottom of the lake. What happened was an accident.

However rare, to see death as the end result for experienced BWCA paddlers when they apparently did nothing "wrong" is troubling. Indeed, the possibility of hypothermia is something canoeists need to have at the forefront of all early- and late-season trips to the wilderness, McDonnell explained.

I traveled to Tuscarora on a cold afternoon in April to talk about some of the dangers that come with paddling in the BWCA. McDonnell said the staff makes a point to present the realities of renting a canoe in May or October, regardless of the canoeist's age, gender, or experience while traveling through the canoe-country wilderness.

"We're not trying to scare people," he said. "But we do try to make it clear that the Boundary Waters is both really fun and someplace that can be quite dangerous."

McDonnell and his team rented Cameron, Weeks, and Johnson their canoe for the May 2020 trip. It's not the first drowning or death McDonnell has intimately known in the Boundary Waters. A longtime member of the Cook County Search and Rescue team on the Gunflint Trail, McDonnell said there was not much else that could have been done to keep Cameron from being dealt the hand he was. "He had his life jacket on, so it's a tough one to point to one thing and say they should have done this or should have done that. Sometimes things happen out there and it really is as simple as just understanding this place can be dangerous, particularly in May. Cold-water drownings scare me more than anything else up here," he said.

Aldritt and his friends decided not to travel beyond Tuscarora Lake on the day they assisted Weeks and Johnson and alerted the authorities as to what had happened. They set up camp on a site within view of the island. Early that afternoon they watched as a rescue squad arrived in canoes and assisted Weeks and Johnson. After the campsite was cleared, the squad led the two men out of the wilderness. Not long afterward, a floatplane found Cameron's body, and Aldritt watched as it landed, loaded a body and a canoe, and then took off again.

McDonnell said Aldritt and his group handled the situation like compassionate people who understand the wilderness is a setting for community. "There's a responsibility as a human . . . to help, but they went above and beyond. It was a very serious situation. But those guys, they were pretty much textbook. They helped out the two guys who were still alive, and they went for help. And they got help fast."

McDonnell said guests at Tuscarora frequently ask about what they should do if they encounter a situation in the BWCA where a stranger needs help, similar to the scene Aldritt and his paddling partners came upon in May 2020. "People will ask what they should do if you're on a portage, and you come around the corner, and there's a guy lying there with a broken leg. If you don't have a way to contact the outside world and someone needs help right away, we tell people that if you're on Seagull [a popular and easily accessible lake], or someplace like Knife Lake, or even Tuscarora, go paddle from campsite to campsite asking for help. In this day and age, you're going to find someone with a device."

If an emergency beacon or cell phone are not options, McDonnell said the second thing to do is to paddle out and get help. "If you have even a general idea of getting around in the Boundary Waters, and you're moving without your gear, you can get out fast." McDonnell said there's an "unwritten code of the wilderness": you help others when they're in need.

"You do it," he said. "Your plans for a trip are put on hold the moment you encounter someone in distress. That's the way it is."

II

Ben Merry was overwhelmed with all the options.

"It had been a few years since I'd been up to the Boundary Waters, and I just didn't remember there being so many routes and lakes and places to choose from," he said. "The hardest part of planning the whole trip was, 'Where do we go?'"

Eventually, he was able to make some decisions. Keep it simple; the kids are coming, he reasoned. Later, on that trip in 1987, while sipping the first cup of camp coffee, Ben stared at a new map he'd purchased the day before in Ely. His family's canoe outfitter suggested getting to Ensign Lake and doing day trips from there. Setting up a base camp was a good option for the young paddlers, the outfitter advised.

Now, on the second day of the trip, Ben was excited to be back in the BWCA. Ben's eight-year-old son, Michael, as well as Ben's older brother, forty-two-year-old Fred Merry, and his thirteen-year-old son, Brian, were also part of the adventure. The group had two aluminum canoes they'd rented from the outfitter in Ely. This was the first time Michael and Brian were sitting in the bow and paddling. It was the first time they helped power the trip.

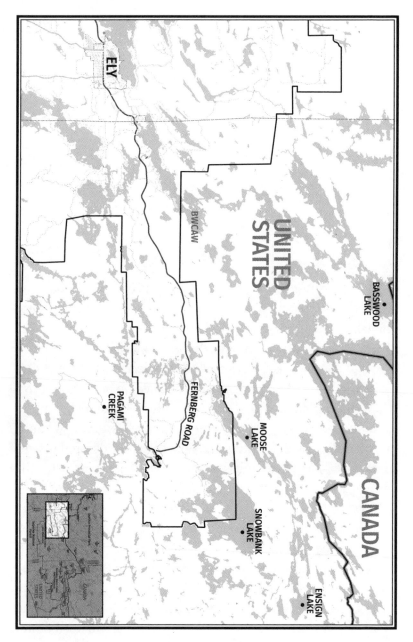

The Merry family camped on Ensign Lake.

Energized by youth and sunny days, the Merry brothers were grateful to be back not only in the BWCA but also in Minnesota. Though they had spent a portion of their lives in the North Star State, this trip was their first to the iconic wilderness since they'd graduated college, gotten married, and started families of their own. They'd both moved away from Minnesota during the previous decade to pursue careers aligned with their education. Fred relocated to Florida. Ben found steady work in Alabama as an engineer. A summer vacation back to Minnesota was years in the making. After everyone's schedules finally aligned, the father-and-son duos traveled together in one vehicle as they motored north across the country. They passed through Tennessee, Kentucky, Illinois, and Wisconsin. They took their time, stopping for ice cream, hamburgers, fuel, and the occasional short walk. They spent one night at a motel in the middle of Illinois but otherwise drove with a steady pace toward Minnesota and the Boundary Waters.

The first day of their canoe trip was a series of getting from Ely to Ensign Lake as quickly as possible. They took a tow through Moose Lake, saving time moving through Newfound and Sucker Lakes before the portage into Ensign. Establishing a secure camp was important to everyone in the group, but most specifically for Michael, the youngest of the foursome. Ensign is a popular lake with easy access: the group considered themselves lucky when they found a prime campsite on the south shoreline. By early afternoon they had set up their four-person Eureka tent near a massive white pine. The concept of a vestibule was not commonplace in the late eighties, but a rainfly of sorts was included with the new tent Ben purchased specifically for the trip.

"It still had the tags and stickers and some packaging stuff in the bag when we opened everything up," Ben said.

Michael and Brian were anxious to explore the area around camp while their fathers continued to establish a base of operations. The boys found interesting rocks in the woods, the stones covered with lichen and soft moss. There were new birds, at least to their eyes and ears, darting from tree to tree. Cedar waxwings. Dark-eyed juncos. Black-capped chickadees. A loon chimed in with its great call. The air smelled fresh, and it was cool and dry.

Meanwhile, Fred connected a green canister to their double-burner cooking stove. Camp now secure, a cup of coffee was in order. Ben sat in a small camping chair and pulled out the map of the area surrounding Ensign, their home for the coming week in the BWCA. They could take the routes up to Vera Lake the outfitter had mentioned, or possibly go over to Knife Lake to gaze into its clear waters and marvel at its towering pines. Another option, one the outfitter did not suggest, caught Ben's eye as he studied the map. It was a creek, possibly even a small river, that spilled from the south end of Ensign toward Boot Lake. The waterway provided other options as well, funneling to the southeast near Gibson Lake. Traveling this route surely would make for an adventure, thought the former Minnesotan, who was thirty-three years old during this particular trip to the Boundary Waters.

"The first day in had been so easy that we thought it would be okay to push it pretty hard that second day," Ben said. "It was my idea."

That first night in camp, the team feasted on hot dogs cooked over the campfire. They passed around a bag of potato chips to complement the main course. The modest campfire kept the boys busy while Fred and Ben casually enjoyed a happy hour beverage. There was some rain in the forecast, but the mood in camp was relaxed and good.

The wind picked up the next morning, but the group was protected by natural structures around their campsite. Windy or not, day two became challenging once the narrow strip of flowing water heading toward Boot Lake entered the equation. The "rather difficult" day trip from camp Ben planned for the group turned brutal in a hurry. Rather than navigating through what appeared on the map as a narrow, winding river, the foursome lugged their two canoes through muck and over beaver dams. Dead cedar and balsam hanging over the creek made for slow progress. Some fallen trees were piled on top of each other in zigzagged stacks. Others came to rest alone, resembling those mechanized crossing arms found at railroad intersections all over the nation that tell people to do one simple thing: stop. Instead of a Huck Finn type of adventure in which the group would float down a creek, the slow progress, along with swarms of mosquitoes, made for a bushwhacking nightmare. At various times along the way there was not enough water in the creek to float the canoes, meaning the travelers had to get out and drag the watercrafts through the shallows. After suffering for hours through thick stands of alder and uneven, spongy terrain, the four ambitious paddlers had to simply turn around and go back to where they came from.

"It took us all day, and we basically never went anywhere," Ben said.

The day trip was a bust. They did not see any wildlife. There were no opportunities to fish. The physical labor required to move through the drainage and its many swamps was unbelievably taxing. After returning to camp late that afternoon, the group, exhausted and hungry, fell mostly silent. They struggled to find the energy to consume dinner, let alone prepare a reasonable meal. The four ate noodles with olive oil and "some seasoning" added to it, Ben recalled. Before the sun went down, the two youngest members of the party, Michael and Brian, were in the tent and ready to shut down their bodies. Fred put liquid soap in the heavy steel pots and dishes. He washed them back in the woods not far from camp. He rinsed them again at the water's edge.

As the afternoon transitioned into evening, the Merry brothers noticed dark clouds rolling in from the west. After a tiring day, there would be no sunset to capture their attention. The loon and other birds were no longer calling. The woods were dark and silent.

"Looks like rain," Ben said.

Lacking the energy to gather firewood, and with rain coming their way, Ben and Fred opted to call it a night. They packed away their food and any stray gear. What was once distant thunder grew louder as it crept closer to Ensign Lake, rolling claps booming above the Boundary Waters. Cloud-to-ground lightning resembling electric rivers lit up the horizon. The men crawled through the small entrance to the confines of the tent. They took off their wet boots and socks. A day of slogging through swamps and over beaver dams had made everything from the knees down wet. It felt musty in camp. A quick change into dry garments was their final task. Darkness was just settling in as the last rays of light held on, mixing with flashes of lightning. Ben closed his eyes. He thinks Fred was talking to him as he drifted off to sleep, though he can't recall if that was only a dream.

"We were so dog-tired I just don't remember much about those final hours from the night," Ben said.

What he does remember is waking up the next morning wanting a cup of coffee.

"I woke up thirsty," Ben said, more than thirty years later. "It felt like I hadn't slept well. I can best describe it by saying that I just wasn't feeling great."

Ben opened his eyes and saw Michael sleeping next to him in the tent. His son was snoring, or at least breathing heavily. Next to Michael was his cousin, Brian, and farthest from the door was Fred. All three of the other canoe-campers were lying on their backs.

It was light outside the tent, so Ben knew the group had been asleep for many hours. The sun does not set until well past 9 PM during the summer months in the Boundary Waters. Since the group crawled into their tent before darkness fell, Ben assumed they'd been resting for at least ten hours, perhaps more.

It had rained for part of the night, at times heavily. Even though their tent was new, some moisture had managed to sneak inside. Coupled with the wet clothing from the day before, the inside of the tent was humid and damp. Ben's sleeping bag was wet to the touch.

Looking to quench his thirst, and not wanting to disturb the other members of the party, Ben slowly and quietly got dressed and made his way outside the tent. His boots were still wet. The sun was out. An eerie stillness had settled over the campsite.

"It was pretty quiet around the whole lake," Ben said. "Not much was happening."

As he started to move around the campsite, Ben noticed his arms and legs felt like they were asleep. His limbs strangely tingled as he clumsily ambled about. He figured it made sense: he'd slept so hard and for so long that his body was feeling somewhat numb. Being stationary in the tent for nearly half a day's time will do that, he reasoned. However, Ben also noticed that he was having a hard time concentrating. He could not make sense of the cookstove, including getting it lit, an elementary procedure he'd done hundreds of times in the past.

"I couldn't light the damn thing," he said. "Normally, that would have made me laugh. But I was just feeling groggy and kind of out of it."

Ben decided to crawl back in the tent and wake up his brother
to assist with the morning routine. The boys would be hungry,
Ben knew, and having breakfast ready would keep the group from
starting the new day with pleas for food. Avoiding a repeat of the
disastrous day trip from yesterday was essential. Ben wanted to
right the ship, and that involved starting out with a good breakfast and lots of coffee. But he needed help. Ben unzipped the tent
and crept in. He kept his boots on this time, moving slowly on
his hands and knees through the entrance and across his sleeping bag. He reached over the boys and tapped his brother on the
shoulder to wake him up. There was no response. He reached
out again, pushing harder on Fred's shoulder. His brother did
not stir. Fred's eyes stayed closed, and there was no movement.

"Fred?" Ben whispered.

Nothing.

Ben crawled deeper into the tent. He was now looming over
Michael, his knees gently touching his son's torso. The physical
contact caused Michael to exhale. The sound he made was strange,
"like a low moan," Ben said. He slapped his brother across the
face to wake him from a presumably deep slumber.

"Fred," he said loudly.

"Fred!"

There was still no response. Michael continued to make a
series of unusual sounds. Fred and young Brian did not stir even
though Ben was now shouting. He shook his brother violently
and slapped him again. Nothing.

He knew Fred and Brian were dead.

"Right then, after all that hollering, that is when I knew," Ben
said.

They'd been struck by lightning. Somehow Ben knew what had
happened. There was no gas inside the tent from a cookstove or

any other such device, so they had not been poisoned from toxic gas. They did not suffocate. They did not have heart attacks. They had been struck by lightning. Ben looked down at his son. Michael was contorting his body into an almost fetal-like position. The boy continued to moan and gently wail.

Ben considered the possibility that his son's life was in jeopardy. He pulled Michael from his sleeping bag and carried him to the lake's edge near their canoe. Michael dangled awkwardly while his dad walked with as much purpose as he could muster. Both canoes were stashed up a small draw, away from the lake. They were overturned. The canoe Ben and Michael had paddled on the trip rested fifteen feet from the lakeshore, the stern intentionally hung up in some thick shrub-like plants on land. Knowing the previous night's storm might arrive with strong and gusty winds, the Merry brothers pulled the heavy canoes into the plants for safekeeping. The canoe made a loud bang when Ben turned it over onto the keel. He dragged the aluminum watercraft to the water's edge. He went back to the shrubs and picked up a paddle and a life jacket. He put the life jacket on. Michael sat up for a moment on the rocks near the shoreline. He was very pale.

"Dad?" he said.

Ben lifted his son and put him in the canoe. His other memories from camp that day are cloudy, but he recalls putting a life jacket on his son. In the canoe, Michael did not sit up but went horizontal, his head resting under the bow seat. Ben climbed in the canoe and started to paddle away from the campsite. He did not know where to go, though he knew getting away from camp toward civilization was paramount. Michael needed to see a doctor. Ben's head throbbed through the entire ordeal.

Ben paddled the canoe west toward the portage that brought them to Ensign. There were campsites and other people near that area of the lake. He worked hard, making slow and arduous progress. After thirty minutes of paddling, Ben approached an opening on the shoreline. It was the portage out, the way home. In that moment, a group of six canoeists was just entering Ensign. One member of the group, a college-aged man from Minnesota, called out to Ben.

"Are you okay?" he asked. "What happened?"

Ben was not aware of how he looked, though his appearance stood out immediately to the other campers. His hair was wild and his eyes were bloodshot. He looked sick and confused.

"Do you need help?" the stranger asked.

"My son needs a doctor," Ben said. "I think we were hit by lightning."

Two members of the party said they would go back to Moose Lake and get word to anyone with a communication device that a father and his son were sick and needed help.

"My brother too," Ben said. "And my nephew. They're back at camp. They didn't make it. They're both dead."

III

Nataly Yokhanis wakes up every morning knowing that the person she loved—indeed, the person she planned to marry—died before he turned thirty.

Similarly, Ben Merry spent most of his adult life with the haunting image of his brother and nephew lying dead in a tent in the Boundary Waters. The memory is there, almost a living thing, waiting to enter his thoughts.

And so, they grieve. Grieving is a process, and through it, several questions remain for both Yokhanis and Merry: Why did these people they love die in the Boundary Waters? What about this place caused them to die here? Does the BWCA have anything to do with it, or was it just their time to pass on? Objectively, there are no answers.

Every year, people die in the woods and waters across the United States. The *Washington Post* reported in 2015 that "somewhere between 120 and 140 people typically die at national parks each year, not counting suicides," according to numbers maintained by the National Park Service. The *Post* noted that those numbers may seem high, "but consider that roughly 280 million people visit the parks each year. That means that if you go to a national park, your odds of dying there are roughly one in two million." Similar to in the Boundary Waters, the leading cause of death in the National Park system is drowning. Also similar to statistics in the BWCA, a 2008 analysis the *Washington Post* shared of park fatality data found that "men accounted for 75 percent of park deaths in 2003 and 2004. And people in their 20s and 50s accounted for more than half of all fatalities."

Billy Cameron was twenty-nine when he died in the BWCA. Fred Merry was forty-two and his son was thirteen when they were struck by lightning and died on the forest floor. These were all young men in a wilderness full of young men. Their ages, it seems, and knowing how much life each person still had to live only make their deaths more challenging to understand. Some look to faith or religion as a means to find a greater purpose in death. In particular, people want to find meaning in the deaths of those who die young. They work to find the link on which to attach valor, significance, or reason. Eventually, one has to accept that when someone dies suddenly or unexpectedly it was likely due to bad decisions, bad luck, or some greater force beyond basic comprehension. Life comes, and it goes. It's a march toward the end, the whole process. Every day, millions of people drive automobiles seventy miles per hour or faster down concrete roads. Rarely do they think about the fact that only a metal frame and some rubber is keeping them safe. Delicate threads keep people alive. The human body can be resilient, but it is far from invincible. Ultimately, life is a temporary experience of occupying space on this planet. Each person who is alive today is going to die. Their death could even happen tomorrow.

These are realities Nataly Yokhanis grapples with on a daily basis. Not long after Cameron's death, as her grief intensified, she sought counsel from a therapist near her home in Dayton.

Talking to a professional about her mental health is something she says has been pivotal in her life without Cameron. "My brother came and stayed with me in Dayton for a couple weeks after everything happened. And I was doing okay in that period," Yokhanis told me in July 2022. "But when my brother went back to Indiana, and I was by myself, it got pretty rough. And that's when I started doing some therapy."

Yokhanis met with the therapist once a week for about three months. She said the therapist was pleased with how the sessions were progressing, but Yokhanis can admit she was taking the notion "fake it until you make it" to a place that wasn't natural, or even healthy. "I stopped seeing a therapist after basically getting told that I was doing okay. And then, a while later, I felt like I was almost taking a few steps backwards. I just didn't really feel like I had dealt with a lot of my emotions. I think I was convincing myself like, *Yeah, you're fine. You're healed.* I was trying to ride an almost false sense of security. And then I think I finally had a moment where I was like, *Okay, you haven't really dealt with all your grief; you've just been trying to put it on the back burner, put it on the back of your mind.*"

Yokhanis returned to therapy. It gave her perspective on "this place that I felt so strange about all of a sudden." That place, the one she learned to fear, was the Boundary Waters.

Researchers at the University of Minnesota Duluth observe that "the grieving person will likely experience many changes throughout the grieving process. The stages of grief are usually categorized as shock, suffering, and recovery." Yokhanis said the shock phase was "instantaneous" when she learned of Cameron's death. It would intensify when she thought of the cold, deep water that took Cameron's life. Whereas most people who think of the Boundary Waters are likely to conjure images of large pine trees, stunning sunsets, casual campfires, and the possible chance encounter with a moose, Yokhanis's mind now goes to a darker place. "I don't blame the lake, or I don't blame Minnesota," she said. "I associate the Boundary Waters with the place that Billy lost his life. And that's about all I think of when I see pictures now from his trips and things like that."

A 2008 study by two researchers from the University of London analyzed what sections of the human brain were activated when participants viewed photographs of things they hated. When the participants saw an object that stirred sentiments of loathing, "several areas of the brain became activated: the medial frontal gyrus, right putamen, the premotor cortex, the frontal pole, and the medial insula. The greater the reported hate, the more these areas were activated," according to the report. But the researchers also discovered the brain activity associated with feelings of hatred displayed patterns similar to those that people exhibit internally when they experience romantic love. "The results surprised us," the researchers noted. In that sense, the feelings, at least neurologically speaking, that move through Yokhanis when she now thinks of the Boundary Waters as a place of death would be similar to those Cameron felt when he paddled a canoe through the wilderness, frolicking in his happy place.

Yokhanis was planning a trip to the BWCA in the summer of 2022, but it never materialized. Logistics, and perhaps a pain still too raw, ultimately prevented her visit. Because she was never drawn to the outdoors in the same way Cameron was, Yokhanis said she is not sure if a trip to the Boundary Waters is something she'll ever get around to doing. In a place where canoes decorate the water, the experience could be too much to process, she admits. "I think it's almost like a subconscious reaction now, but if I see videos of people kayaking, or people in boats, I kind of have this reaction now to it that I used to not. I realize how dangerous, and how fatal those things can be. I see someone in a canoe or kayak and think that if something were to go wrong, somebody could get really hurt, or even die. It used to be that I would see people on a boat or whatever, and see people are having fun, I just thought they were enjoying their time. And now I look at it and think, you know, things can go wrong."

Spending many of her nights alone since Cameron's death, Yokhanis said it's almost as though she has lived two lives. "I had this life that I lived that Billy was a part of," she said. "I had very strong future plans, and like this trajectory of my life that I saw with him that I was living, and then that timeline, that part of my life, that version of my life, that ended."

Dry drownings are rare in the BWCA. Most of the canoeists who drown in the Boundary Waters are not wearing a life jacket when they die. Wearing a life jacket increases the chances of survival if a canoe capsizes and people enter the water. Few would dispute such a claim. However, some people, like Cameron, still die even when they seemingly do everything right. In October 2012 Thomas and Cynthia Pineault, a married couple in their fifties, died on Alton Lake in the BWCA. Alton is a popular body of water not far from the Sawbill Lake entry point. The Pineaults were very familiar with this area of the Boundary Waters. Despite their experience and the fact that they were apparently doing what they should be doing, they were last seen alive on a windy day on Alton. The next day, Thomas and Cynthia were found floating in the water. They were wearing life jackets, and they were dead. In a subsequent media report, officials from the Cook County Sheriff's Department said winds in the area and a drop in temperature could have played a role. Local authorities said Thomas and Cynthia had been floating dead in the water for at least twenty-four hours when they were found by another group of canoeists on a trip in the wilderness. It took equal parts bad weather, cold water, and bad luck to kill the Pineaults. The same unique and challenging circumstances took Cameron's life as well. Life jackets can help someone in cold water, but nature still reigns supreme.

Over the course of two years, Yokhanis found the strength to embrace a new version of herself, she said. It took therapy, acceptance, and dealing with a lot of pain to get there. Her journey continues with the knowledge that others have died in the Boundary Waters. And more people will in the future. Yokhanis said she sympathizes with anyone who has lost, or will lose, a loved one in the BWCA. "Someone, at some point, will die on a canoe trip in the Boundary Waters again," she said. "That's heavy. It's a really sad thing to think about."

Canoe trips start out as adventures. Sometimes they turn deadly. Yokhanis wakes up every morning knowing this truth. And still she rises. "This is a new chapter, or a new part of my life, and I have to continue to live it," she said. "I can't hold on to that old life so much. And I know Billy would have wanted that for me. He wouldn't have wanted me to essentially never try to find happiness, or find love. I know he would have wanted me to continue on and be successful and hopefully find someone that would be a good person for me. And so, I think when I started feeling like I could feel things for other people, that was my sign to myself like, *Okay, you are ready. Try to take it slow and just see how it goes.* I don't put expectations on things anymore. Nowadays, I'm just very much about, if it works out, it works out. If it doesn't, it doesn't. Life goes on. I think it actually made me better in the end."

IV

Ben Merry sat alone on the steps outside a small church in Coleraine, Minnesota, on the day of his brother's funeral. The sun
was out. There was almost no wind. Funeral attendees ushered
past, some nodding, others allowing the grieving brother the
space he clearly needed. When the proceedings started inside,
Merry refused to enter the church.

"I guess I didn't want to go in for the funeral. I just sat there on
the curb outside the church and thought, *You know, Fred doesn't
want to be in there,*" Merry said. "And I wasn't all emotional about
it. I just decided he didn't want to be there and I didn't want to
be part of him being in there."

Coleraine is a nugget of a municipality tucked next to a series
of small towns on the edge of Minnesota's iconic Iron Range.
Bob Dylan's childhood hometown of Hibbing is about thirty
miles away. Ely, the canoe capital of the world, is about a hundred miles to the north. The funeral for Fred and his son, Brian,
was held in Coleraine about a week after they were struck by
lightning.

Their deaths were quick. At their campsite in the BWCA, a
large pine stood just west of the tent, its roots and branches

spreading out like ancient veins and growing tentacles. One of the roots ran just beneath the surface of the earth. Small sections of the root were exposed entirely, to the sun, the wind, and the elements. The root extended more than ten feet from the trunk of the tree. The campers pitched their tent on the edge of this root. After the tent was standing, the root made a ridgelike formation on the floor. The protrusion was so minor it did not grab the attention of Ben and Fred and their boys. The root was on the far side of the tent, away from the lone entrance the group members had to crawl through to get inside. Fred and Brian slept on this side of the tent, with the partially exposed root positioned beneath them. No one mentioned the protruding root following the first night sleeping in the tent. On the night of the storm, a bolt of lightning struck the pine, ran down the root, and killed Fred and Brian almost instantly.

As Ben Merry sat on the steps of the First United Church of Coleraine in the small Minnesota town where his brother and nephew were about to be buried, he kept his thoughts distant from what was happening behind him. In many ways, his refusal to enter the church was the beginning of decades of suppression. It wasn't until I called Merry more than thirty years later asking for information that he said he started to think about seeing a therapist to process what occurred during their 1987 trip to the BWCA.

"I thought about that, especially after we talked," Merry told me in September 2022. We first spoke in spring 2021, after I found a newspaper article in the *Orlando Sentinel* from July 24, 1987. In the piece, a reporter for the *Sentinel* describes in detail what happened to the Merry brothers and their sons in the Boundary Waters. Ben was unfamiliar with that particular article, though he knew some articles had been written shortly after the lightning strike. The story made the Orlando paper because Fred was a resident of the suburban community of Maitland, Florida, at the time of his death. Other news articles were published in Minnesota, along with Fred's and Brian's obituaries.

Of all the people I spoke with for this book who knew someone who died in the Boundary Waters, Ben Merry stands, emotionally speaking, in a class of his own. Each time we talked, Merry expressed very little of the grief, pain, and sometimes disbelief that others carried. "The whole thing didn't hit me hard," Merry said of the deaths. "It still hasn't. It never will. I'm just not made that way."

A skinny southerner with a gray goatee, Merry was born and raised in Minnesota but spent most of his adult life in Georgia. He's in his sixties now, and the idea of outdoor recreation no longer interests him, at least not with any degree of motivation. In 2022 he did take a trip to Crater Lake National Park in Oregon, but he's done with backcountry camping, he said. Though he expressed little emotion during our conversations, I asked Merry what impacted him the most about the lightning strike and his brother's death. "The worst thing was that my mom had to find out," Merry said. "She set out to screaming when she got the news, which is about what you'd expect. It was hard to choke down. I was so sad that had to happen to her."

Though Ben and his son, Michael, survived the ordeal at the campsite in the Boundary Waters, the lightning strike showed little mercy to the survivors. Both Ben and Michael were knocked unconscious at one point shortly after the strike. When Ben staggered about the campsite the morning after the storm, he was suffering from a concussion. Michael, just eight years old at the time, was delirious, indeed barely alive, from the electricity that went through his body. Ben had a red stripe that ran from his upper leg to his neck, a temporary scar that was essentially a burn. His right eardrum was destroyed, literally blown out from the blast of the bolt. His ability to see was affected as well. Six months after the incident, Ben lost vision in his right eye. Years later, a lens transplant eventually helped restore most of his sight.

Based on first impressions, the canoeists who discovered Ben Merry as he desperately paddled out of the wilderness likely thought they had come across a living ghost. The reality is their assumptions weren't too far off. The sclera of his eyes, typically what one refers to as the "white" of an eye, had transformed to a disturbing shade of red. When the others saw him, Merry's hair looked unkempt in the way "Unabomber" Ted Kaczynski's did when authorities arrested him inside a dirty cabin in Montana. Essentially, Merry looked like a madman. "We didn't have a mirror or anything like that at camp," he said. "But I can recall they were pretty stunned when they saw me paddling up to that portage."

According to the National Weather Service, lightning strikes kill about forty people annually in the United States. Hundreds more, possibly thousands, die across the planet each year after being struck by lightning. Such data is hard to keep in the remote corners of the world where cell phones, the internet, and local governments are not always established. What is known is that, on average, about forty million lightning strikes hit the ground in the United States each year, according to the National Weather Service. A comprehensive study the National Park Service prepared on wildfires and lightning states, "Lightning is described as having two components—leaders and strokes. The leader is the probing feeler sent from the cloud. The return streaks of light are a series of strokes that produce the actual lightning bolt or flash that we see." Fred Merry and his son were killed by a "leader," before any humans caught a glimpse of the bolt.

In addition to the forty who die, an average of 240 people are injured by lightning each year in the United States. Still, the odds of being struck by lightning on a trip to the Boundary Waters are less than one in a million. Even if you do get struck by lightning, 90 percent of all strike victims survive, as was the case for Ben Merry and his son. According to the National Center for Environmental Health (NCEH), an arm of the federal Centers for Disease Control and Prevention, certain factors can put you at greater risk for being struck by lightning, including most forms of outdoor recreation. Near the top of the list is canoeing and kayaking. In other words, the Boundary Waters is a place where death by lightning strikes will continue to occur so long as people continue to recreate there. At the first sight of lightning or sound of thunder, the NCEH recommends "to get off the water immediately, because you may not know which way the storm is moving, or if a 'quiet' area of the storm will start to generate lightning."

A person in a canoe on the water is typically the tallest object around. This reality increases the probability that the canoe, or the person inside the canoe, will be a strike point. Cook County sheriff Pat Eliasen said in a canoe on a lake in the Boundary Waters is arguably the last place you want to be in a lightning storm.

"Lightning is a real danger to canoeists," he said. "It absolutely needs to be taken seriously."

Getting off the water is one thing, but most lightning strikes reported in the Boundary Waters take place on land. For example, a single bolt of lightning knocked four young women unconscious during a severe storm in 2016. The teenagers, part of an

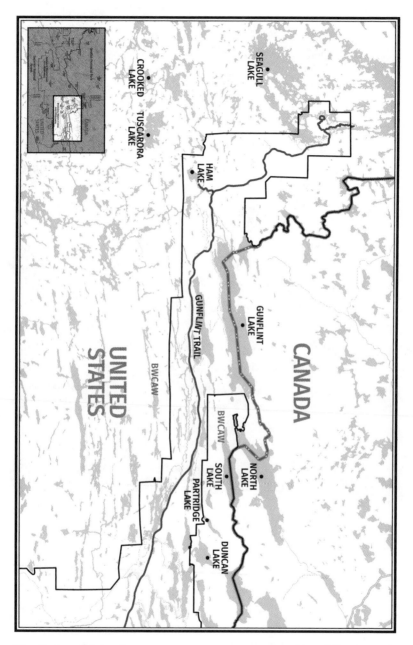

The Outward Bound group encountered severe weather while camped near Crooked Lake.

eight-person canoe party, were less than a week into a twenty-eight-day canoe trip through the organization Outward Bound. The group had set up camp on an island on the massive Crooked Lake near the Canadian border. As they enjoyed an evening outing, a sudden and very powerful wind from an oncoming storm made it too difficult to safely paddle. They quickly made it to land on the expansive border lake. According to reports from officials in St. Louis County, "the group was practicing lightning safety by sitting on life jackets to provide insulation between themselves and the ground. However, lightning struck the trees about 120 feet away and traveled through the root system to where the campers were located."

Local officials involved with the rescue later told the *Timberjay* newspaper in Ely that "the lightning bolt struck a large white pine about 100–150 feet away from where the group was riding out the storm. The blast stripped the tree of branches, blew 2×4 width chunks of wood from the trunk and even blew bark off of nearby trees. The force of the blast also threw one of the girls in the air in addition to knocking four of them unconscious. Most of the other girls, ranging in age from 14–16, also suffered fairly extensive second degree burns to the backs of their legs and buttocks."

After the lightning strike, the leaders of the Outward Bound group used a satellite phone to report the incident and to request immediate medical assistance. Treacherous conditions on the water made it impossible for a helicopter or a motorboat to reach them. Officials had to wait until early the next morning, when a floatplane met the group near Sunday Bay. Emergency personnel "brought the five most injured girls out first, and transported them to the Ely Hospital, where they were admitted for observation. Another girl and one of the adult leaders came out in a second evacuation, leaving one of the group leaders behind to wait for recovery of all of the gear by another Outward Bound party," according to a report from the St. Louis County Sheriff's Department.

About thirty minutes before a lightning strike literally blew up a pine tree and electrified the Outward Bound group on Crooked Lake, the same storm system ripped along the border lakes just north of the Gunflint Trail. On Duncan Lake, one of the most popular spots on the eastern side of the wilderness, straight-line winds snapped numerous trees, including a towering white pine that landed in a campsite on the lake's western shore. The falling tree killed the brother of Minnesota governor Tim Walz, who was a congressman at the time of the incident. The governor's brother, Craig, died on Sunday, June 20, which happened to be Father's Day.

I was live on the airwaves from the Grand Marais radio station, WTIP, early the next morning. In our news report, we talked at length about the previous night's storms. Included in our reporting was a memo from the Cook County Sheriff's Department that said "43-year-old Craig Walz of Rochester, Minn., was with his son and two other camping partners when a large pine snapped and landed in the area where they were camping. Law enforcement officials were notified at 10:25 p.m., and staff from nearby Camp Menogyn helped the two unhurt campers rescue Jacob Walz." Jacob, the governor's nephew, sustained significant injuries from the falling tree.

In 2018 I interviewed Governor Walz about the incident that took his brother's life. It is the only interview in which Walz specifically answered questions about his family's painful connection to the Boundary Waters and is among only a handful of times the governor has ever addressed the topic publicly. As we spoke of the BWCA and about his brother's death, Walz said, "First of all, Joe, our family will be forever in debt to the entire community." He continued, "Folks, strangers, saved my nephew's life, risking their own in the middle of the night in a storm. And we are deeply appreciative of that. And we're also heartbroken. Craig was the center of our family. He and I paddled the Boundary Waters for decades. He loved that place. It gives me some comfort to know that's where he rests. It's an important place. It's an important place to Minnesota. It's deeply ingrained in us. I took teams up there to build camaraderie and to bring together sports teams from high school. We introduced a lot of kids over the years for their first time to the Boundary Waters. But if you want to see what the best of Minnesota looks like, it happened on a stormy Father's Day in 2016. And because of what they did, my nephew Jake is going to live a good and happy life because of those folks."

The unfortunate bond shared between Governor Tim Walz and Ben Merry is that both of their brothers died in the BWCA. A tree fell on the governor's brother and killed him almost instantly. Lightning took the life of Ben's brother, Fred. Three decades separate the two events, though the outcomes are the same.

In 2022 I asked Merry what he thinks about wilderness travel and where it fits in with everyday fears people have as they move about the earth.

"People are so different now," Merry told me. "People are so risk averse, afraid of anything that's going to happen to them. And later, what's going to happen to their kids. You can't live your life being afraid of everything. That's just crazy. And now, everybody's got to have mental health care and all of that. And yeah, some of that could be good. But it just makes me feel like people feel [they] are obligated to protect themselves and their family from everything. And that's just nuts. People get killed going to the Boundary Waters, yeah, but you might get killed on the way home too."

V

About a month after the Father's Day storm that killed Craig Walz and injured several others, another massive storm raged across the Boundary Waters. On July 21, 2016, authorities confirmed two people were killed by falling trees on the Canadian side of Basswood Lake in Quetico Provincial Park. Basswood sits in both the BWCA and Quetico.

The two people who died were thirty-nine-year-old Nickie Rorth Lac and thirteen-year-old Christian Sanchez. They were part of a Boy Scout group from Texas camping in the canoe-country wilderness. In addition to the dead, two other members of the group were injured during the storm. The injured campers were flown out of Quetico and to a nearby medical facility the next morning. For health care workers on the edge of the Boundary Waters, the arrival of an injured canoe-camper through the emergency room doors is simply part of the job.

North Shore Health, the small hospital in Grand Marais, is a place where dozens of injured, bleeding, confused, and, on rare occasion, dead canoeists from the Boundary Waters end up. The hospital is an unassuming place. A glowing, electric fireplace greets visitors who arrive via the large main entrance on the southwest corner of the building. Though the hospital was renovated and remodeled in 2018, its central artery has the feel of a small-town doctor's office. It's the type of medical place one might expect to find near the edge of a wilderness, particularly when compared to much larger hospitals in Duluth, Minneapolis, or Rochester. Lake Superior, the moody and powerful force that, as the Gordon Lightfoot song goes, does not give up its dead, sits four blocks below the Grand Marais hospital's front door. On the building's backside is the less inviting emergency room. This is where most people who are injured in the Boundary Waters enter the facility. According to North Shore Health officials, between 2015 and 2022 about fifty people who sustained injuries in the BWCA were brought to this typically quiet health care facility. Their injuries ranged from bleeding wounds caused by the poor swing of a hatchet to a gashed forehead following a tumble onto jagged boulders lining a portage trail. Paddlers who had an allergic reaction to biting or stinging insects may join others with sprained ankles, twisted knees, broken arms, separated shoulders, and all manner of cuts, scrapes, and bruises. A fairly common injury involves barbed fishhooks that land deep in someone's hand or, worse yet, their face. Most of the people who come to the emergency room are white men who talk sheepishly about their injuries. And then there are the dead. Those with nothing more to say.

When someone dies in the Boundary Waters, local law enforcement or a medical professional calls family members of the deceased. These are typically short, unpleasant conversations. On the eastern side of the Boundary Waters, Dr. Kurt Farchmin, who worked as the director of the medical staff at North Shore Health from 2015 to 2023, placed several of these calls during his tenure at the Grand Marais hospital. Farchmin acknowledged that, generally speaking, the calls were challenging.

"It's especially rough for people who had come up here from out of town, or who are not local people," Farchmin said. The idea that someone came on a vacation to the Boundary Waters and died in the process is not the type of news a spouse or parent wants to hear.

When it comes to these calls, Farchmin said there's no easy way to deliver the news. "In my experience, it's just being direct," he said. "And it feels blunt, but to just say that, 'I'm really sorry to tell you, but this person in your life has died.'"

Medical professionals and, more often these days, law enforcement officials in Ely and Grand Marais who make these phone calls provide the context and circumstances that led to an individual's death, Farchmin explained, and that's about the extent of the information that is shared. "You just cut to the chase and let people start to process. As you're talking to people, you can hear it settle in. Oftentimes there is a pause, and then people get more distraught as you talk, because it's settling in what you're telling them."

Farchmin recalled making a phone call to the family of a man who drowned in Pine Lake on the far eastern edge of the wilderness in late fall 2016. At that point, Farchmin had been on the job for about a year working as a health care provider in Grand Marais. The man who died on Pine Lake was fifty-nine-year-old Michael Hickey, a Duluth resident who frequented the BWCA. Pine Lake is a deep lake with a reputation for being a wind tunnel. It stretches for more than seven miles east to west, with just over eighteen miles of total shoreline. More than one hundred feet deep, it's often rolling with dangerously cold water. Hickey, a dedicated BWCA angler, likely had little chance of survival when he capsized his canoe on a cold day in November. It took authorities several days and the use of highly advanced sonar equipment to locate his body. Farchmin made the call to Hickey's family to share the news of the death. In a situation like that, Farchmin said, when the person is reported missing and it takes a couple of days to recover the body, there's almost a sense of relief to the conversation. "It's still pretty terrible though," Farchmin added.

Looking at a dead body when someone drowns in the Boundary Waters, from a medical perspective, is not particularly jarring. "In fact," Farchmin said, "they can seem really quite peaceful. There's no other trauma; there's nothing else that happened." In a car wreck, for example, a person can be disfigured, with smashed limbs or appendages. With a drowning, the body is together. The figure remains whole. "There's an obvious change; you can just see that there's not a life in that body anymore," Farchmin told me in November 2021. "It seems like a weird thing to say, but they look peaceful."

Farchmin was thirty-one years old and fresh out of medical school when he started working as a physician in Grand Marais in 2015. He received his medical degree from the University of Minnesota Duluth. He completed his residency through the Center for Family Medicine in Sioux Falls, South Dakota. Having grown up in Duluth, he was very familiar with the BWCA and Quetico. Farchmin moved back to Duluth in 2023 after practicing medicine in Grand Marais for just shy of a decade. His family is full of dedicated canoe-country wilderness travelers, particularly his father, Jon Farchmin.

At the time Kurt Farchmin was hired, Cook County still used a physician as its primary coroner. Farchmin said examining the bodies of people who died in the BWCA, making the phone calls to family members, and seeing the number of people who come in injured started to reshape the way he viewed the wilderness. "There was a period of time where I started to think that taking a canoe trip, going in there, seemed like a big liability," he said. "I was like, *Wow, that's where people go to die.* And when you see the worst of it, you start to question some of what this place can do to people."

When things go wrong in a wilderness setting, effective communication between search and rescue responders, law enforcement, and the people who are in distress is paramount. Rick Slatten from the St. Louis County Rescue Squad takes that notion a step further: after the operation is complete, he says, accurate information in the media is a key component of how the public perceives search and rescue operations. Take, for example, a lightning strike from 2019 on Knife Lake in the BWCA that left a group of seven Girl Scouts from the Chicago area and their pair of young-adult supervisors frightened and in need of medical attention. The Girl Scouts were between thirteen and seventeen years old. Their counselor, who went by the name "Chocolate Chip" around camp, was twenty years old, as was their guide from Northern Lakes Girl Scout Canoe Base, Madelyn Fahnline.

Following the incident, initial media reports said some of the scouts were "critically injured" after the lightning strike. The overnight effort by the St. Louis County Rescue Squad to get the Girl Scouts to safety gripped the attention of Minnesotans, even prompting an 11 PM tweet from Governor Tim Walz that read: "A group of very brave Girl Scouts need your prayers tonight. They're waiting out dangerous conditions and potential injuries in BWCA, while search & rescue teams try to locate them. Our first responders train for this. We're going to do everything we can to bring them home safe."

After the rescue took place, the Girls Scouts organization, attempting to downplay the situation, took to any media platform that would share their perspective. The reason, presumably, was to minimize the public's intense reaction to information about young girls camping and getting injured in the woods under the supervision of the Girl Scouts. "None of the Girl Scouts or guides who were rescued from a remote Minnesota island near the Canadian border overnight was injured by lightning, contrary to initial fears," the *Pioneer Press* newspaper in St. Paul reported soon after the original story made headlines across the Midwest.

Slatten, the captain of the St. Louis County Rescue Squad, told me in 2021 that he was disappointed the media were so quick to jump on board with the narrative that the rescue was essentially not a big deal, that the young scouts were not at risk, and that the scout leaders were only following standard protocol for reporting an incident. Only the *Star Tribune*'s Tony Kennedy got it right, Slatten told me. In an August 3 article, Kennedy wrote: "There was nothing ambiguous about the distress call from a campsite full of Girl Scouts who experienced lightning last weekend deep inside the Boundary Waters Canoe Area Wilderness (BWCA). Two of the six scouts were in pain and one of them had lost all sensation in her left leg. She felt tightening in her jaw and rated her pain an eight on a scale of one to 10. Those clarifying details, recorded in the 911 command log kept by the Lake County Sheriff's Office and described by an official who helped field the original call, drew an apology Friday from the Girl Scouts regional spokeswoman, Nancy McMullen. She initially described the situation in far milder terms by saying that some girls merely felt 'tingling' and no one was injured."

I spoke with Fahnline in October 2023 about the incident. She is an experienced BWCA paddler: the trip with the Girl Scouts was her seventeenth time on Knife Lake. She said when the lightning hit their camp just after 5:45 that afternoon, it was like an explosion.

"I remember watching the lightning come down. And then I really viscerally remember the feeling of the thunder, which was just so loud," she said. "It made my ears hurt so bad. And it also just kind of felt like something had grabbed my sternum, and shook it really violently. It was this feeling of my bones rattling."

After the bolt hit the campsite, Fahnline fell backward. Despite the initial setback, as the leader of the group of seven scouts, she almost immediately sprang to action to check on the teenage girls. Five of them had clearly been impacted by the lightning, Fahnline observed, though she later came to understand it was from ground current moving up through their legs, not a direct strike. Nonetheless, one of the scouts said she saw electricity come through her fingers after the current moved through her body, Fahnline told me. Another scout said she lost all feeling in one of her legs after the lightning strike.

It took approximately seven hours for the search and rescue team to evacuate the scouts. Fahnline spoke with law enforcement and search and rescue personnel from St. Louis County about the situation, sharing details about the experience from the campsite. One of the people she spoke with was Slatten.

Almost immediately afterward, Fahnline said she was instructed by officials from the Girl Scout organization not to comment publicly about the situation. In the days after the incident inaccuracies appeared in published accounts, and Fahnline grew frustrated that she wasn't allowed to share details about what happened. This frustration simmered for two years, with Fahnline eventually opting to take action: she signed on with the St. Louis County Rescue Squad.

"I wanted to get involved," she said.

Fahnline officially joined the rescue squad in 2022. And there she became reacquainted with Rick Slatten.

Slatten is an expert on finding missing people. He's been doing this work for decades, most of it in and around Lake Superior and the Boundary Waters. The St. Louis County Rescue Squad, the largest and most advanced of those covering the Boundary Waters region, consists of ninety-five highly trained volunteers from northeastern Minnesota. These people are interested in helping canoeists and others who get into bad situations in the woods or on the water. A dominating figure, Slatten has a deep voice, broad shoulders, and a thick Minnesota accent. Despite decades on the job and his best years long behind him, Slatten is not the type of guy you want to mess with. His hands are weathered from the sun and from frequent exposure to cold wind and water. His muscular shape still reflects the hard work he engages with on a daily basis. In addition to being the captain of the largest search and rescue squad that works in the Boundary Waters, Slatten travels the country educating people—mostly other search and rescue organizations and law enforcement agencies—on how to find humans in the woods, regardless of whether the missing person is dead or alive.

Slatten told me numerous times over a couple of years of communication that the media are often too quick to get a story published before all the facts are in. As someone who often reports on the happenings in and around the BWCA, I countered by telling Slatten that in a newsroom we're working with minimal information from responding agencies, and there is, for better or worse, competition in the news industry to get a story posted first. "Many journalists are competitive people," I told him. Slatten said he can appreciate the work the press does in sharing information about search and rescue operations in the BWCA and across northeastern Minnesota. Regardless, when an organization like the Girl Scouts, the Boy Scouts, or a canoe outfitter attempts to spin facts or downplay situations to fit a certain narrative and the press take the bait, it makes Slatten's blood boil.

In this case, Slatten said McMullen's media interviews caused confusion and made the public question if responders and law enforcement "overreacted by launching a dramatic, midnight run through a thunderstorm to evacuate the scouts," as Kennedy reported.

Slatten said the way the Girl Scouts shared information about the incident after the fact was confusing, if not stupefying. "You had girls who experienced electrical current," Slatten told the *Star Tribune* in 2019. "We're going to move hell and high water to get in there and get them taken care of."

Lightning strikes and drownings are not unique to the BWCA. People die in the woods and in the water all over the globe. In the United States, there's an abundance of data on things like the total number of deaths and injuries for the country's sixty-three national parks. An abundance, at least, when compared to any similar data for the more than eight hundred designated wilderness areas spread across the nation. The National Park Service, under the Interior Department, is different from the US Forest Service, which operates under the umbrella of the Department of Agriculture. The Park Service keeps fairly strict information on who is coming in and out of places like Yellowstone, Yosemite, Glacier, and the Grand Canyon. In a place like the Boundary Waters, people fill out self-issued permits between October and April or on day trips during the bulk of the canoe season. It's a simple form, completed at a kiosk somewhere on the edge of the wilderness. Nobody checks an ID; there's no currency exchanged. For overnight trips between May and September, visitors to the BWCA register online for a permit or obtain one directly from the Forest Service or a wilderness cooperator.

In comparison, at a national park visitors often engage with a ranger at a drive-up kiosk before entering. In general, it's easier to know who is coming and going at a national park than in a wilderness area. It's therefore easier to track the data when someone dies. For example, in 2022 the National Park Service received 312 million recreation visits. Among those many millions of people, 204 of them died.

In the sense that every backpacker in Yellowstone or Glacier National Parks has some remote chance of being mauled and killed by a grizzly bear, so too could every canoeist who enters the BWCA die from a lightning strike, by having a tree fall on them at their camp, or by drowning. All of these things have happened in the BWCA during the past forty years. Still, Farchmin said he quickly got over the "I'm afraid to go there; I might die" mantra that had seeped into his consciousness after performing medical examinations on people who died during their trips to the Boundary Waters. If he followed his own logic, Farchmin reasoned, he should be terrified to drive a car after performing an autopsy on someone who died in a traffic accident. Or, perhaps even more outrageously, he should be afraid to get old after studying the body of a local man who died from heart complications at the age of ninety-two. Farchmin came to understand that, ultimately, everyone is going to die, and there's not really a reason to be afraid of such a truth. "Death is a part of life," he said. "I've grown to be a firm believer that the riskiest thing you can do is not take risks. That's what stretches us; that's what helps us be healthy."

Furthermore, Farchmin explained, the gamble that you could, on a very remote chance, die in the Boundary Waters only adds more intrigue to an already exciting adventure. "That's part of why we go there, right? It's because we know on some level that this might not be safe. I think that's the draw for some: to test yourself. To find out, *Can I survive out in the wilderness for a period of time and maybe enjoy it?*"

Farchmin, who is skinny, wears glasses, and keeps a neatly trimmed red beard, said his fear of recreating in the canoe-country wilderness returned for a short period in 2019 following the death of seventy-one-year-old Craig Sicard of Minnetonka, Minnesota. Sicard died of congestive heart failure in Quetico, not far from the Cache Bay Ranger Station and the park's iconic Falls Chain, a series of rapids and waterfalls that drops from the southeast corner of the park toward Kawnipi Lake. Sicard died on the scene, and it was the only dead body the longtime Cache Bay ranger, Janice Matichuk, ever saw during her thirty-five years in the park. The others were either in body bags or taken from the park before she arrived on the scene, Matichuk told me in 2018.

The news of Sicard dying from a heart attack on a portage made Farchmin wonder if his own father, Jon, would face a similar fate on his next canoe trip. "My first thought was like, *Dad! Don't go out there. That could happen to you,*" Farchmin said. "And then I'm like, *Heck no, Dad. Go out there!* I mean, my dad could have a heart attack pushing the lawnmower. We can't just always be in fear about what might happen. We shouldn't stay away from a beautiful place just because something bad might happen."

PART II

Still Out There

I

It's easy to get lost on foot in the Boundary Waters. In a canoe, which is by far the most popular means of travel in the BWCA, there's usually some reference point that will get you to where you want to go. It could be an island, a landmark, or a spot on the map that registers. Even on a large lake like Seagull or Saganaga at the end of the Gunflint Trail, or Basswood and Lac La Croix near Ely, certain indicators usually emerge to guide the way. When you're trying to navigate in the Boundary Waters, it's easier to have an "aha moment" on the water than it is on land. A primary reason it's easier to get lost in the woods than it is on the water comes down to one factor: visibility. The boreal forest encompassing the Boundary Waters is a maze of brush, balsam, cedar, spruce, and pine. Here, in the thick timber and dense alder, it can be challenging to see more than ten feet in any direction. Those who step off a portage trail or stray from a campsite will quickly encounter swamps, bogs, and an uneven ground dotted with all manner of boulders and rubble. Some of the rocks are slick, rounded, and covered with moss. Others are jagged and make the ground uninviting, as though designed by nature to keep people out.

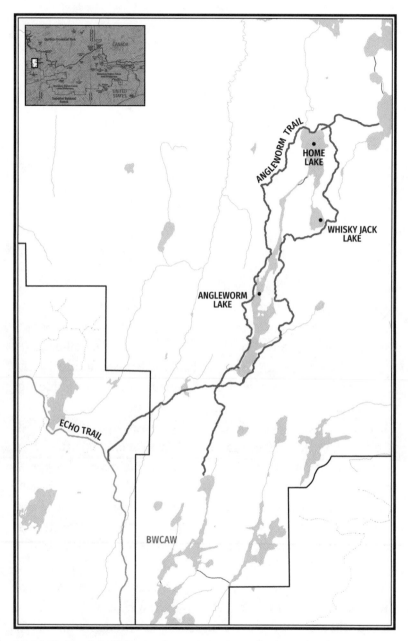

Lloyd Skelton hiked the Angleworm Trail to Whisky Jack Lake.

Lloyd Skelton knew about this type of terrain. An experienced outdoor adventurer, he knew the Boundary Waters well. Over the course of decades, Skelton made countless trips to the BWCA from his home in Minneapolis. A versatile and accomplished athlete, Skelton enjoyed kayaking, canoeing, and hiking in the BWCA. It was a place where he felt completely alive and connected to his core values. Camping, lots of water to explore, expansive wilderness—the BWCA had it all.

One afternoon in June 2005, Lloyd Skelton took off most of his clothes near a campsite in the Boundary Waters and walked into the woods. He never returned. Skelton, who was fifty-eight at the time, vanished. After multiple searches, including extensive ground operations involving cadaver dogs, Skelton's body has never been found. Skelton's skull is still out there somewhere in the Boundary Waters.

Skelton was a skinny guy from Minneapolis who liked to drink, smoke, and play outdoors. He was also a chess player who gathered with friends in the Twin Cities to celebrate and share the experience of mental fortitude via the chessboard. His passion, though, was for the wilderness. And he was experienced. Skelton once paddled from northern Minnesota to Hudson Bay, a feat most BWCA adventurers, even those who frequent the wilderness, will never accomplish. He climbed mountains across the American West and had a network of friends who similarly shared his passion for the outdoors. All in all, if somebody wanted to put a label on Skelton, it would be easy to call him an "outdoorsman."

"Dad loved taking these types of trips," his daughter, Lisa Skelton, told me. "He liked the ones where he just kind of took off and would let come what may."

On June 2, 2005, Lloyd left Minneapolis northbound for Ely and the Boundary Waters, a four- to five-hour drive. He'd recently lost his job at the architecture firm HGA. Skelton told his family the firm was "downsizing," but Lisa wonders what role her father's drinking might have played in the unexpected loss of employment. Understanding that the term "problem drinker" is subjective, Lisa said her father had become one in his final years, occasionally smelling like alcohol early in the morning. Regardless, a trip to the BWCA was perhaps exactly what Lloyd needed to reset, to plan his next steps in life. There had already been talk of retirement in the near future, so additional time for adventures was a welcome invitation for Skelton regardless of the circumstances that led to a loose daily calendar. The month of June, for example, was a playbook of opportunity, Skelton reasoned. The lakes in the Boundary Waters were ice-free. The bugs were coming on, but the days were long and the nights still cool. In a broad sense, everything in life is about timing and circumstances. For Skelton, his decision to head to the Boundary Waters in June 2005 proved to be fatal, for reasons that likely will never be fully understood.

Skelton arrived in Ely to lousy conditions. It was rainy and cold. A stiff wind continually blew in from the north, keeping the temperatures in the forties during the day, dipping into the thirties at night. A sense of warmth from the sun didn't visit the north woods for days. Everything was damp. This weather is not uncommon for early June in northern Minnesota, but it's not what most would consider ideal conditions by any means, particularly for a water trip in the BWCA. After attempting to ride out the poor conditions for two nights in and around Ely, Skelton opted to temporarily abandon his idea for a paddle trip. Instead, he'd take to the trails. On June 4, Skelton filled out a free, self-issued permit to hike the Angleworm Trail. The popular hiking route is located about seventeen miles from Ely off the Echo Trail.

The Angleworm Trail is a roughly thirteen-mile loop that wraps around the long and skinny Angleworm Lake. It is an entry point to the BWCA, though canoeists who choose this route face a 716-rod (2.2-mile) portage to start their trip. For most, as it was for Skelton, this is a hiking trail. It's also a gorgeous route. The trail cuts through stands of red and white pine, follows a stunning ridgeline overlooking Angleworm, and features a steady diet of elevation change. The trail is challenging in some sections but well maintained and easy to follow. About five miles from the trailhead is Whisky Jack Lake. A picturesque BWCA lake, Whisky Jack is roughly thirty-five acres in size, fairly shallow, and surrounded by pine, spruce, and balsam. The occasional birch and cedar also dot the shoreline and surrounding forest. A lone campsite is tucked in on the lake's southeastern corner. Granite outcroppings at the campsite create ample and outstanding views to the north. Though small compared to many lakes in the BWCA, Whisky Jack is nothing short of charming.

After arriving at the Angleworm trailhead parking lot, Skelton started to weave his way through the woods. He didn't carry much gear for his hike. He did not have a day pack, a water bottle, or anything to eat. Most of the possessions he brought with him to Ely remained in his van, law enforcement later discovered. The stretch of cold, wet weather kept many hikers and paddlers away from the woods and water to start the month of June that year. There were no reports of anyone seeing Skelton on the trail on the day of his permit or in the following days. What is known is that something happened to Skelton near Whisky Jack Lake that compelled him to strip off his clothes and wander into the woods. It's likely Skelton spent his final moments staggering about in the dense forest of the Boundary Waters. How far from Whisky Jack Lake and the Angleworm Trail Skelton traveled before he died remains a mystery.

Lisa Skelton didn't report her father missing until late in the day on June 14, nearly two weeks after he left Minneapolis for Ely and the BWCA. Lisa said there was nothing unusual about her father being gone on an extended solo trip with minimal communication to friends and family back home. In addition, when things were going well in the woods, Lloyd had a tendency to drag out a trip longer than originally scheduled. Lisa also wondered whether she had the date of his return wrong, thinking her father meant he would be back Tuesday, June 14, not June 7, as she originally thought. However, something seemed off. Not long after Lisa called the authorities in Minnesota to report her father missing, the search for Lloyd Skelton in and around the Boundary Waters began.

Finding someone in the BWCA without knowing where the person strayed from their course is an arduous task. Once Skelton was reported missing, it was anyone's guess as to where exactly he might be. He had not filed an overnight entry permit for the BWCA with the US Forest Service. If he was in the canoe-country wilderness, he could be on any number of trails, portages, or lakes spread across the 1.2-million-acre Boundary Waters. Without a lead, it came down to checking various parking areas, trailheads, and entry points on the edge of the wilderness. Authorities also scoured a collection of campgrounds, Ely motels, and trailheads from the Echo Trail to others along the Highway 1 corridor to find Skelton, or at least his van. On June 16 his vehicle was located at the Angleworm trailhead. The ground search could begin. Among those responding to the search and rescue operation were Rick Slatten and the St. Louis County Rescue Squad.

As they gathered at the trailhead, the crew didn't know what Skelton's plans had been. His kayak was still fixed to the top of his van, so it was likely he'd left on foot. Crews trekked to the north on the Angleworm Trail with the hopes of finding Skelton alive.

"We don't know what was going on in Skelton's head when he walked in there," Slatten told me in December 2021. It took the search and rescue team several hours of walking to reach the campsite near Whisky Jack Lake. Not long after they climbed a modest ridge leading up from Angleworm Lake toward Whisky Jack, a member of the search party found Skelton's jacket. The jacket was tightly rolled and carefully placed near a large boulder that sits along a spur trail leading from the Angleworm Trail to the campsite at Whisky Jack. Moments later, the team discovered Skelton's pants and socks several hundred yards south on the trail heading back toward Angleworm Lake. According to a report filed the day of the search by local authorities, Skelton's pants looked as though they were rolled down haphazardly and then "stepped out of." His shoes were never found. Inside the pants were Skelton's wallet, the van keys, and a lighter. No other articles of clothing, possessions belonging to Skelton, or anything that could be called "evidence" was ever found.

The case remains unsolved—one of the few the St. Louis County Rescue Squad has been involved with where the file is still open. "This troubles me," Slatten can admit. By now, Slatten said, whatever remains of Skelton has been returned to nature. Whatever bones weren't eaten by animals have been swallowed by moss and years of fallen leaves that morph into duff.

Tom Brown Jr. is an American author and survivalist who operates what is referred to as a "tracker school" in New Jersey. Basically, many of the people who follow his teachings want to learn what it takes to survive in nature if they're left to their own devices. Slatten says it's possible Skelton set out on the Angleworm Trail to get rugged and embrace some of this ideology, though it's not likely. Another possibility is that Skelton walked into the woods with the intention of never coming back. "Was he going in to commit suicide? Or was he going in to play some Tom Brown Jr. thing dressed barefoot in a loincloth and try to live in harmony with nature?" Slatten asks. "It's unlikely, but I don't know. It's speculation. We'll never know."

Iris Vilares is a cognitive neuroscientist and an assistant professor of psychology at the University of Minnesota. She investigates how humans make decisions and how these approaches differ in people with psychiatric and neurological diseases. One area of particular interest for her is how people make decisions during times of uncertainty and how these processes are represented in the brain. Skelton was alone and likely distraught as he wandered into the wilderness. I asked Vilares what Skelton's brain was likely experiencing in the moments that led up to his disappearance. Vilares immediately mentioned the amygdala, a cluster of almond-shaped cells located near the base of the brain. Humans have two of these clusters, one on each side of the brain. As part of the limbic system, this portion of the brain is responsible for a person's emotional and behavioral responses. The amygdala also activates the fight-or-flight response, which is the brain's way of helping people in immediate physical danger react quickly for survival purposes, Vilares said. When things are going really badly and the possibility of death is a serious consideration, something known as an "amygdala hijack" will occur. This is where the amygdala "begins to shut down the frontal cortex and we stop thinking rationally," Vilares explained. Skelton likely faced some sort of panic state in his final moments as he stripped off his clothes near Whisky Jack Lake. By that point, Vilares said, Skelton's brain wasn't functioning properly, "including the pathways to logic and rationality."

The brain is a complex organ. It does amazing things, and it's prone to panic. It can also take an otherwise sane human and make them behave very strangely. One theory concerning why Skelton took off his clothes and vanished into the forest is that he started to suffer from hypothermia. Soon thereafter, it's possible he experienced a phenomenon known as "paradoxical undressing." This is when someone's body temperature drops below ninety-five degrees Fahrenheit and they start to lose their minds. Even though the individual is dangerously cold, they begin to feel warm. In this state, most people take off some or all of their clothes. Given that Skelton's clothes were spread across the Angleworm Trail near Whisky Jack Lake, this scenario may well be what occurred. However, Slatten does not subscribe to the notion that paradoxical undressing is what happened to Lloyd Skelton in the Boundary Waters. In fact, he's quick to distance it as a possibility in most instances. "That's so overplayed. At least in my experience," he said of authorities labeling a situation as paradoxical undressing. "Someone finds a mitten on the ground and, 'Oh! He's hypothermic and undressing!' No, maybe you just dropped [the mitten]. But you know, with Skelton, here's a case where it could be, but I'm not going to go so far as to say that's what it was."

I first learned about the strange phenomenon of paradoxical undressing in 2006 when I was a twenty-three-year-old news reporter in Oregon. The story I was working on involved a family from San Francisco who got lost on their way home after spending Thanksgiving in Seattle. My first job out of college was at the *Curry Coastal Pilot* in the small town of Brookings, situated a few miles from the California border on the Oregon coast. Though I moved to Bend, Oregon, shortly before this story broke, I was well connected with officials in Curry and Josephine Counties in Oregon, which is where this family ended up lost while trying to take a shortcut to the coast. The Kim family, including thirty-five-year-old technology reporter James Kim, his wife, Kati, and their two young daughters, left Seattle the day after Thanksgiving in 2006 bound for Portland. After spending some time there, they continued south down Interstate 5 with a plan to reach the small town of Gold Beach, located on Oregon's southern coast. The family had reservations at Tu Tu' Tun Lodge near the Rogue River and the Pacific Ocean. However, as they attempted to take a shortcut to Gold Beach over the rugged coastal mountains of Oregon, the family's Saab station wagon became stuck on a remote road. They spent the next week trying to survive. They kept their vehicle running as the temperatures dropped close to freezing at night. When they ran out of gas, they used the car's battery until it too died. Next, they burned the vehicle's tires and huddled around the flames for warmth. As snow continued to fall and the temperatures dropped, the ordeal dragged on in the southwestern Oregon wilderness, among the most isolated pockets of the nation. This area is easily as remote and rugged as the Boundary Waters, perhaps more so.

James and Kati ate almost nothing during the days they spent lost in the woods. They rationed baby food and crackers for the daughters. For water, they all drank melted snow. Kati nursed both of the children for supplemental nutrition. One of the daughters was four years old at the time; the other a mere seven months old. As the situation deteriorated, and only when it appeared nobody was coming to rescue them, James Kim set out on foot. Five days later his body was discovered in about eighteen inches of freezing water in Big Windy Creek. He was lying on his back, wedged against a fallen tree in the creek's steep canyon. Before locating his body, authorities first found Kim's pants lying in a patch of snow near the rim of a canyon, not far from the creek.

They later found other articles of clothing he shed as the depths of hypothermia set in. After he had walked for nearly twenty miles through the unbelievably challenging mountainous terrain, Kim's body gave out less than a mile from a lodge. Even though the facility was closed for the season, it was fully stocked with supplies. Meanwhile, Kati Kim and the couple's two daughters were rescued by a helicopter two days after James left the vehicle.

The image of James Kim lying mostly naked and dead in the cold creek haunted me as a young journalist. Strangely, I was also captivated by the story. I frequently thought about Kim and his journey through the wilderness. It seemed like something out of a movie. His death took place within a relatively short drive of where I lived at the time, another aspect that captured my attention. These woods where I recreate, I came to understand, are not a place to underestimate. If you're not prepared, you can die out here. This became a new way of thinking when I traveled or adventured. And considering that late fall and winter were my favorite times of the year to be outside, the Kim case had an added layer of personal connection.

Dr. Cameron Bangs, an Oregon physician widely viewed as one of the nation's leading hypothermia experts, told the *Oregonian* newspaper in 2006 that "it is common for someone stranded for a long time in cold weather to start paradoxical undressing." Bangs said that when someone's core temperature drops below ninety degrees, various systems begin to fail. The result, Bangs told the *Oregonian*, "is that warm blood moves toward the skin and a person begins to feel hot. You become confused and behave in a strange manner. You feel too warm and you start shedding clothes."

It took search and rescue teams a week to find Kati Kim and her two daughters, and another two days to find James Kim bobbing face up and dead in the creek. In Skelton's case, it took offi-cials involved with the search two days after they started looking for him to find his clothes near the Angleworm Trail. It's likely Skelton died several days before the authorities found his cloth-ing, possibly more than a week. It's not likely he died near the clothes, or the cadaver dogs the team deployed would have been alerted by the scent of blood or a corpse. Even if scavengers like wolves or a bear found his body and dragged it away, there would have been more evidence to support such an event. This means Skelton shed his clothes and wandered into the woods, away from Whisky Jack Lake and the Angleworm Trail. He did this under his own power, consciously or not.

I asked Slatten if the inability to find Skelton's body is among the most troubling of his storied career in search and rescue response efforts. After pausing for a moment, Slatten said *trou-bling* isn't the right word, but Skelton's case is among the most confusing.

"I think about Lloyd's case a lot," Slatten told me. "I don't think about it from the PTSD perspective though, but from a solving-the-mystery perspective. Why did Lloyd do this? You know, what was going on in his head? And then you play it out from there. . . . Most of us, our feet are not conditioned to walk bare-foot in the woods. You get bloody and hurt in a hurry trying to, because we're tenderfeet."

Decades after Skelton's disappearance, his body, if it is in the BWCA, has likely been returned to the earth. Despite the pas-sage of time, Slatten says he remains curious as to what hap-pened to Skelton's shoes. "We got his socks, but did he put his shoes back on? We never found the shoes. Did he run around naked in a pair of tennis shoes? We don't know. And so, I'm curious how far he made it."

II

Lloyd Skelton's sister, Roseann Lloyd, is a poet and well-known writer in the Twin Cities. Roseann was close to her brother and spent time with him the day before he left for what proved to be his final trip to the BWCA. They had breakfast together at the Birchwood Cafe in Minneapolis, though during the meal Lloyd wasn't hungry and "barely ate anything," Roseann said. The two opted not to drive to the Birchwood, even though Roseann was not able to walk at the time due to a ruptured tendon in her leg. Lloyd gladly pushed his sister in a wheelchair the several blocks to the cafe. Along the way, the two of them shared stories from their childhood, including the time Roseann and her friends tried to convince Lloyd there were lions and other large beasts living in the basement of their childhood home. "Oh, we laughed and laughed on that walk," Roseann said. "I don't know why everything seemed so funny that day. It was just one of those great moments that siblings can share."

In the years after Lloyd's disappearance, Roseann channeled her grief through the written word. She wrote a collection of essays and poetry about her brother titled *The Boy Who Slept Under the Stars*. The poems range from reflective to sorrow-filled narratives. In one poem, titled "But Were You Mad?," she writes: "Hell yes, I was mad. Mad that he left in the afternoon without taking into account his tremor, his cigarettes. Mad at his belief that his luck and stamina would go on forever . . . Mad that he told his buddy at the outfitters that he'd head to the North Shore but didn't. Didn't tell anyone he was heading for the Echo Trail . . . Mad that when the Virginia, Minnesota police put crime scene tape around his trail of clothes, some canoeists hesitate, *Is a serial killer loose in the Boundary Waters?* Mad that people picked up his clothing, that is, evidence. But evidence of what?"

Roseann sent me a copy of the book in August 2021, not long after we spoke about her brother's disappearance and presumed death in the BWCA. She told me about her visit to the Angleworm Trail in 2011, six years after Lloyd went missing. Roseann didn't return to the trail expecting to find anything that would lead to a conclusion about her missing brother. She just wanted to smell the woods of the Boundary Waters again. She wanted to feel the space where Lloyd left his clothes by the side of the Angleworm Trail. It was, Roseann told me, an "attempt to feel something tangible" after her brother had been missing for a half dozen years. As she reflected on the hike years later, what stands out most in her memory is finding the elusive state flower of Minnesota, the showy lady's slipper, near the trail. "The friend I was with said Lloyd sent the flower to me. She said it was a gift from him," Roseann said.

Though not a writer like his sister, Lloyd Skelton was a reader. He appreciated the work of author Bill Bryson, often reading his stories aloud to friends around campfires or back at the cabin after a day of adventure was complete. A passage from Bryson's book *The Body: A Guide for Occupants* talks of death not as a mystery but as the unescapable reality it is. Bryson wrote: "There are thousands of things that can kill us—slightly more than eight thousand, according to the International Statistical Classification of Diseases and Related Health Problems compiled by the World Health Organization—and we escape every one of them but one. For most of us, that's not a bad deal."

I visited the Angleworm Trail and hiked to Whisky Jack Lake in October 2021. With me were my frequent Boundary Waters paddling partner, Matthew Baxley, and Sean Emery, a YouTuber with a channel that focuses on hammock camping in places like the BWCA. Most people know Emery by his nickname, "Shug." The three of us took our time walking the Angleworm Trail as we trekked the five miles to Whisky Jack. All of us had backpacks full of equipment, including hammocks to sleep in, food, and rain gear. Our hike started under clear skies, though we knew rain was in the forecast overnight. We observed sensational fall colors and talked about life and death: what it means to die and the fact that we're all going to experience it. We observed strange mushrooms growing from the forest floor. The three of us listened to red squirrels chatter as they set about in their hysteria of preparation for the coming winter. The forest smelled of wet leaves and damp cedar. The air was rich with the changing of seasons. Still, it warmed up nicely throughout the day. By the time we made it to the campsite at Whisky Jack, we were all drenched in sweat from the inclines and the mildly strenuous walk. At the campsite, Baxley and I immediately stripped and jumped into the lake, indeed showing little regard for our clothing as we stepped out of our pants. Shug stood on the shoreline, somewhat puzzled that his hiking companions were suddenly swimming naked in the cold lake.

The Whisky Jack campsite is perfectly positioned, with a metal fire grate situated near the lake's edge. We had no trouble finding trees to hang our three hammocks. I forgot to bring my rain fly, but we improvised by stringing a large garbage bag over a thin rope tied between two trees, known in the camping world as a "ridgeline." With the knowledge that Skelton was in this very location in 2005, a certain energy found its way into our camp. We weren't afraid; what we felt was a sense of wanting to know more. With our camp secure, I made a cup of Medaglia d'Oro instant espresso and took great comfort in the companionship of my fellow hikers.

On the day Skelton set off on the Angleworm Trail and disappeared, all of his outdoor gear, including his packs, food, water bottles, and camping supplies, were left in the van. Slatten said this struck him as unusual, given that the round-trip hike to Whisky Jack Lake is about ten miles. And while it's not the same type of excursion as summiting a mountain in the Tetons, it's nothing like a casual stroll around Lake Harriet in Minneapolis either. Slatten said there are whispers of suicide in Skelton's case. Ultimately, what happened to Lloyd Skelton in the Boundary Waters will likely never be solved. His death will forever remain a BWCA mystery, a tale shared by generations of canoe-campers and hikers in the nation's most-visited wilderness area. Mystery aside, the thing that stands out to Slatten about this death is that Skelton was not prepared to be in the woods on the day he went missing.

"Within the context of Mother Nature, of it being harsh, going in unprepared is a bad idea," Slatten said. "Skelton's got all this stuff, and it's in his car. He had gear, and he elected not to take it. He's five-and-some-change miles over extremely rough terrain back in the Boundary Waters with zero gear. Things happen back there: a windstorm comes through, blowdowns happen, thunderstorms kick up. Trails get obstructed. And I don't go much farther than the pit toilet without my day pack on. You never know what's going to happen."

III

Every summer, people get lost in the Boundary Waters. In September 2022, Jennifer Fitzer, a resident of Golden Valley, Minnesota, joined their ranks. After walking away from her campsite and becoming disoriented, she spent a rainy night alone in the BWCA near the Gunflint Trail. This was the fifty-six-year-old Fitzer's first trip to the Boundary Waters.

According to a law enforcement report from the Cook County Sheriff's Department and subsequent conversations I had with Fitzer, she became lost while exploring near the Rib Lake campsite in the early afternoon on September 8, 2022. After her internal compass led her astray, she walked north for several miles through thick forest and various swamps. She eventually made it to Dawkins Lake, which is located south of Extortion Lake and just west of the Banadad Ski Trail, not far from the paved and popular Gunflint Trail. After arriving at Dawkins Lake, Fitzer found a large floating log and essentially rode it along the shoreline, thinking she was still on Rib Lake. Ultimately, she spent the night in the woods wearing only a T-shirt and thin, outdoor-style pants. She got some restless sleep near Dawkins Lake, wondering about bears, moose, or other animals she might encounter. She did not have food and ran out of water during the night.

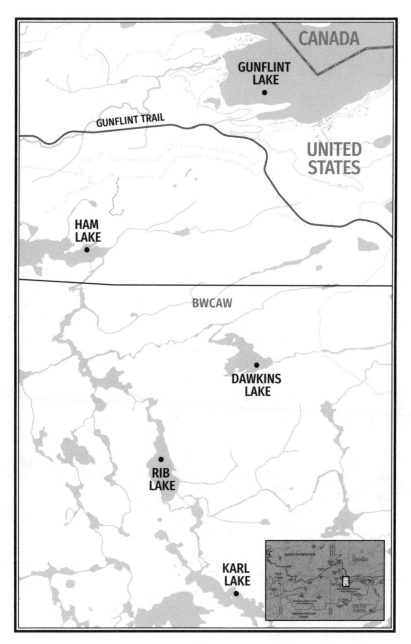

Jennifer Fitzer was lost in the wilderness between Rib Lake and Dawkins Lake.

Meanwhile, back on Rib Lake, Fitzer's brother, Chuck, and others in the camp became worried when Jennifer was gone for more than an hour. After scouring the area, the group discovered they had cell phone reception. They dialed 911 and connected with dispatch in Grand Marais at the Cook County Sheriff's Department. Members of Cook County Search and Rescue were deployed in the late afternoon and traveled via canoes to the campsite. With daylight fading by the time they reached Rib Lake, the search party determined it would be most effective to initiate an aerial and ground search the next morning at first light.

On September 9, while ground crews searched on foot and from canoes, a Beaver floatplane searched from above. The pilot located and rescued Jennifer Fitzer from Dawkins Lake around 9 AM. She'd spent a soggy, cold night in the woods. She was suffering from the early stages of hypothermia when she was rescued by the floatplane. The plane took her to a nearby lodge, where medical personnel tested her vitals and learned more about what happened. After warming up at Gunflint Lodge, Fitzer was released and essentially escaped the entire ordeal unharmed.

About a week after this all went down, Fitzer and I connected by phone. She told me what stands out the most to her from the experience of wandering in the woods of the Boundary Waters is the thickness of the forest once she strayed from the Rib Lake campsite.

"It was unlike anything I'd ever seen," she said. "I mean, of course, there's no trails. You have to go over trees and around trees. When you step down you end up in a swampy area covered with moss, and then you trip over something and fall flat on your face. And there's branches slapping you, and again, it's like nothing I've ever seen before. Everywhere else I've ever camped, it's always groomed trails and not dense forests like this. So, yeah, it was tough going."

〜〜〜

Not all who go missing in the Boundary Waters are rescued so quickly, or found so easily. Some sit for days waiting to be rescued. They ration food, try to stay warm, and more or less hope for the best. Others, like Skelton, are never found. The skinny chess player from Minneapolis is not the only person to meet such a fate.

In September 2004 a Minnesota college student named Nathan Williams traveled to the Boundary Waters for a fall hunting and fishing trip. Unlike Skelton, not a trace of Williams has ever been found. No human remains. No clothing. And there's no reasonable explanation as to where he could be.

Williams, twenty-one years old at the time of his disappearance, was a student at the University of Minnesota Morris. On September 28, 2004, Williams drove a 1966 Ford pickup truck that he and his father remodeled years before from central Minnesota to Superior National Forest. The truck was later found near Hog Creek, on the edge of the BWCA in Lake County. The vehicle was unlocked when authorities discovered it parked along a Forest Service road several days after Williams departed his college campus. Former Lake County sheriff Carey Johnson told the *Duluth News Tribune* that no remains were ever located and nobody came forward with or offered information about what happened to Williams in the wilderness.

As is customary when people go missing in the BWCA, a multiagency land, water, and air search set out to find Williams. The search parties scoured a nearly six-mile radius from where the truck was parked near Hog Creek. Similar to Skelton's case, cadaver dogs were brought in, presumably to find a corpse or a skeleton, but they never picked up a scent. Search parties took to canoes and put underwater cameras in some of the water bodies where Williams might have gone but found nothing of interest. With search parties discovering no leads, it appeared to them as though Williams literally vanished.

"It's as if he was here one day and then dropped off the face of the Earth," said Jim Beauregard, then chief of the Morris Police Department, in a 2007 interview with the *News Tribune*.

Dave Williams, Nathan's father, made multiple trips to Minnesota from the home he shares with his wife in Maryland in an attempt to find the couple's only son. In a 2007 interview, not far from where the truck was parked, Dave Williams told a reporter from the *Duluth News Tribune* who was following the story: "He sure picked a beautiful place to disappear. This is the last place we know for sure that he was alive. . . . This is a terrible place. But it's also the last connection I have to my son."

Not having a human body to bury in the ground or turn to ash brings confusion to the grieving process. It also extends the effort and work required by the responding agencies. Indeed, all human deaths that occur in the Boundary Waters are investigated by law enforcement, according to Cook County sheriff Pat Eliasen. But when someone is not found, it means more work on the ground and possibly air searches. There's supplemental paperwork at every step for the agencies, from a local sheriff's department to the Minnesota Bureau of Criminal Apprehension. Because there was not a single clue that could lead authorities to the whereabouts of Williams, he remains on the state agency's list of missing people.

The sense of mystery stirred by a missing person is essentially the opposite sensation caused by finding a dead body in the woods. And indeed, Eliasen said, people on a canoe trip have found "deceased people" in the BWCA. On most occasions, according to Eliasen, this involves younger paddlers finding an elderly male who was on a solo canoe trip and died of a heart attack. Other times, a group will leave behind someone who dies on a trip, as was the case on Rose Lake in the BWCA in the late 1990s. "The guy had a heart attack, and the people who were with him did CPR on him for hours," the Cook County sheriff explained. When it became obvious CPR was not going to work, the group made the arduous journey back to their vehicle at West Bearskin Lake near the Gunflint Trail, traveling the iconic Stairway Portage and across pristine Duncan Lake along the way. "They had to canoe all the way back out. Because, at that point, there were no cell phones, or even much in the way of satellite phones. They had to come all the way out and get in contact with us. Then we flew in there with a floatplane with the Forest Service."

It would be dismissive to say that only newcomers to the canoe-country wilderness are prone to lonely deaths in the Boundary Waters. Even legends of this storied wilderness can die alone. And perhaps nobody embodies legendary BWCA status more than Benny Ambrose and Dorothy Molter, the last two residents of the BWCA Wilderness.

Many second homes, seasonal cabins, and resorts were located throughout what is now the BWCA for decades up until the passage of the 1964 Wilderness Act. Though the pathway for the BWCA to become a federally protected wilderness started in the 1920s, the restrictions only tightened when the Boundary Waters Canoe Area Wilderness Act was signed on October 21, 1978, by President Jimmy Carter. These federal laws essentially banned anyone from living where people now temporarily camp, paddle, portage, and recreate. While the law banned human habitation in the woods, there were two exceptions: Ambrose and Molter. Both were residents of what is now the protected wilderness prior to the legislation passing through Congress: Ambrose on Ottertrack Lake; Molter on Knife Lake. The two knew of each other but were distant neighbors who enjoyed solitude. It took an outpouring of support, including from Vice President Walter Mondale, a longtime Minnesota resident, in order for Ambrose and Molter to remain in their remote cabins. To make it official, the US Forest Service dubbed them "volunteers in service" so they could continue living in the BWCA.

Ambrose established himself as an icon of the north woods during the half a century he spent in the canoe-country wilderness, including the two decades he continued living near the Canadian border following the federal legislation. He died in August 1982 of a heart attack at his remote outpost. Ambrose was born in Waukon, Iowa, and came, as so many do, to seek solitude in the northland. He spent decades hauling in bags of soil from Iowa and areas of Minnesota so that he could garden near the shores of Ottertrack Lake. Ambrose befriended many from the Gunflint Trail community over the years. And he still died alone.

Similarly, Molter, commonly referred to as "the Root Beer Lady," met thousands of canoeists at the site of her homestead on an island on the pristine Knife Lake. Molter was actually the last resident of the BWCA, passing away alone at her cabin in 1986. She was most widely recognized for the root beer she served at her Knife Lake outpost, selling it until 1964 and the passing of the Wilderness Act. Molter lived on Knife Lake from 1934 until her death more than fifty years later. By the time she died, her fame had moved far beyond the reaches of the BWCA.

Her obituary ran in the *New York Times*, where it read, in part: "Dorothy Molter, once described as 'the loneliest woman in America,' died in a log cabin where she lived for 56 years on a wilderness island, officials said today. She was 79 years old. Miss Molter, the last permanent resident of the million-acre Boundary Waters Canoe Area, was found dead Thursday, officials of the United States Forest Service said."

Although Ambrose and Molter have taken on iconic Boundary Waters status to some degree, neither of them was particularly interested in designating the woods and waters here as a motorless wilderness area. Others were. Famed outdoors writer Sigurd Olson is frequently referenced when people talk about this protected wilderness. And indeed, the effort to preserve this area from logging, extraction, and development was a long road. In many ways the fight to protect this place continues, including, some environmentalists say, from proposed precious metal mines located just outside of the wilderness boundary. However, looking back to that crucial period of 1920 to 1978 and how the Boundary Waters region came to be protected, two names are often overlooked: Arthur Carhart and Ernest Oberholtzer.

Along with famed conservationist and author Aldo Leopold, Carhart was an early architect of what are now classified as designated wilderness areas in the United States. There are more than eight hundred such areas spread across the country. And while Leopold is famous for his writings, including *A Sand County Almanac*, Carhart is not a name that leaps to the forefront for many canoeists who travel through the Boundary Waters. Canoe-country legends like Olson, Molter, or Gunflint Trail icon Justine Kerfoot did more writing in this region, and had more written about them, than Carhart did, and likely ever will. However, Carhart's influence, and a specific journey he took to the Boundary Waters in 1921, literally shaped how the federal government and the American public define designated wilderness in the United States.

The US Forest Service directed Carhart to Superior National Forest in 1921 to tour the area and report his findings to the federal government. They were interested in how the area could best be managed and were counting on Carhart's experience in the backcountry to assist in their decision-making process. During his expedition to the rugged landscape of northeastern Minnesota, Carhart traveled a route from Ely toward what is now the Sawbill Trail area. At the time, he was fresh off a similar expedition to Colorado near Trappers Lake. The Forest Service had sent Carhart to the mountain lake to survey a road that would likely lead to development around the lakeshore. However, after completing the survey, Carhart recommended the Forest Service not build the road, but rather keep the acreage protected and preserved as a wilderness area. During his visit to Superior National Forest in 1921, Carhart came away with a similar recommendation. Leave it alone, he said.

Another person who carried a similar message about the border lakes was Oberholtzer. A curious traveler and artistic storyteller, "Ober," as he was commonly known, first arrived to the Boundary Waters region in the early 1900s. During the summer of 1909, Oberholtzer canoed an estimated three thousand miles with his Ojibwe friend and guide Billy Magee. They explored a tremendous amount of the Rainy Lake watershed, an expanse of wilderness that includes border lakes above the Gunflint Trail, the extensive BWCA to the west, Rainy Lake, and the enormous Lake of the Woods in Minnesota and Canada.

Oberholtzer supported Carhart's "leave it alone" campaign when a timber baron named Edward Backus proposed building a series of dams in the Rainy Lake watershed. Throughout the 1920s Oberholtzer encouraged the Minnesota legislature and the US Congress to protect wild places like the Boundary Waters. It took time, but by 1934 President Franklin D. Roosevelt formed a federal committee that would essentially monitor the happenings in the Boundary Waters region in terms of land management. Roosevelt gave Oberholtzer a key seat at the table, where he could offer an informed local voice. Oberholtzer's appointment by the president followed the creation of the Quetico-Superior Council and the passage of the Shipstead-Nolan Act in 1930. This seldom-referenced law withdrew federal land extending from Lake Superior to Rainy Lake from activities like homesteading and logging near lakes and rivers. The federal legislation also stopped the dams from being built. Furthermore, it served as a pathway for wilderness acts to follow. Without the Shipstead-Nolan Act, the Boundary Waters would not look or feel the way it does today.

Conservationists' tireless dedication to protecting these magnificent wild areas, places like the Boundary Waters, seems to add significance when people die in them. The hard work of Oberholtzer, Olson, and others to preserve the Boundary Waters doesn't align with someone drowning on their summer vacation or fishing trip to the Gunflint Trail. The grandeur of the place makes it challenging to understand death here. It's no less tragic when someone dies in a car accident on Interstate 90 near the Minnesota and South Dakota border. The result, after all, is the same: someone dies. However, there's not a lingering sense of "place" between a paved roadway and someone dying there. In a traffic fatality, the road is simply the location, the spot where the event occurred. When someone dies in the BWCA, be it in a drowning or from a tree falling on their tent, there is typically a connection between the death and the setting. "They died in the Boundary Waters," we say, almost as though the wilderness were somehow responsible.

⌒⌒⌒

Despite the incredible value and importance the Boundary Waters holds for so many people, death is no stranger to this landscape. Speaking with someone who has experienced, or even witnessed, a spouse, sibling, child, or friend dying in the Boundary Waters is a somber task. And I've spoken with many. During a presentation I gave at Chik-Wauk Museum and Nature Center at the end of the Gunflint Trail during the summer of 2021, one of these stories came to life in front of an audience. The tale involved the accidental drowning of a young man, Tom Ackerman, in the Boundary Waters in 2000.

Mark Hargis was in his early twenties when his friend, Ackerman, died on Saganaga Lake at the end of the Gunflint Trail. I wrote about their experience in the book *Her Island: The Story of Quetico's Longest Serving Interior Ranger*, a biography of Janice Matichuk. Hargis, Ackerman, and four others were paddling across the mighty Sag near the Cache Bay Ranger Station when their canoes capsized in a violent windstorm. All six members of the trip entered the frigid June waters of the canoe-country lake. Matichuk rescued five of the men. Ackerman sank to the bottom and died. It took divers two days to find his body. Matichuk told me about the ordeal several times when I spoke with her during the process of writing *Her Island*. She said that, despite the wind, Hargis's desperate screams could be heard from nearly a half mile away. They were primal sounds, she said, the type of noise that can only be associated with death. Ackerman was not wear-ing his life jacket on the day he died. His death, Hargis main-tains, is a motivating factor to do good on this earth. Hargis struggled for years to find purpose in his friend's death. He said Jesus Christ, God, and an unwavering faith carried him through. They still do, Hargis told me in 2020.

And so it came to be that Hargis stood in front of a group of strangers at Chik-Wauk Museum in July 2021 to share his story about death in the Boundary Waters. It was purely a coincidence that Hargis, then in his forties and married with three children, was back on the Gunflint Trail the same weekend I was giving the presentation about the Quetico ranger. About a week before, he'd reached out via email to thank me for writing the book about Matichuk and to say that his family was coming to visit the Boundary Waters area. They had rented a cabin at Tuscarora Lodge and Canoe Outfitters, Hargis explained. In response I told Hargis about my presentation at the museum that weekend, and that he should stop by with his family if he felt comfortable doing so. When he arrived, I invited Hargis to the front of the room. More than fifty people were in attendance.

"You don't want your worst day to end up in a book," Hargis said, fighting back tears.

He was not alone; nearly everyone in the room wept.

Hargis had stood on the rocky slope of an island on Saganaga when Ackerman glided through 150 feet of cold, iron-stained water before reaching the bottom of the deepest lake in the BWCA. Because Ackerman came up for air on two occasions after he was under the water, it's likely he was no longer breath-ing shortly after he went under for the third and final time. The imagery is haunting: a dead college student sinking to the bot-tom of the lake. This event, including Hargis's own terrifying screams of desperation and his helplessness, is now a part of who Hargis is in the world. He told me that losing a friend in the BWCA is something that never really leaves you; all one can do is learn to accept what is. "I don't want to say you ever get over it," Hargis said. "It's more like you learn to make peace with it, or you let it motivate you to lead a better life. That's how I've been able to move forward."

For most people, a canoe trip is supposed to be equal parts challenge and entertainment in the natural world. There's nothing in the playbook about having to witness a paddling partner die. And, like so many other stories about death in the BWCA, Hargis's situation is not entirely unique. For Minnesota resident Elaine Barber, the final images she has of her husband, Richard (Dick), are of watching him drown in Quetico Provincial Park, not far from the US–Canadian border and the BWCA. Experienced paddlers, Elaine was seventy-five years old and Dick was seventy-eight when they set out on their final canoe trip together in June 2013. They were heading for Argo Lake in Quetico, a favorite of theirs and one well known for its clear water and excellent fishing. To get to Argo, among Elaine and Dick's tasks was to navigate a stretch of rapids around the Basswood River. The couple had done this years before without having to portage. This time, however, the river was swollen with snow runoff and early-summer rainfall. As they navigated the surging river on the Canadian side of the border, they went over a steep ledge and capsized. Both of them emerged to the surface of the water. Their pack bags drifted about while Dick and Elaine attempted to gather their composure. Acting quickly, Elaine swam to a rubber pack that held some of their gear, including their tent, their

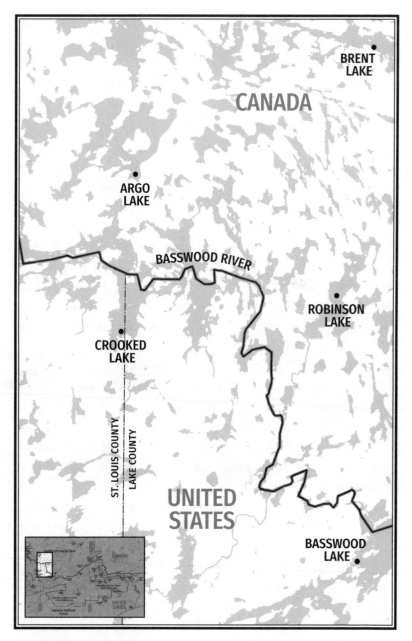

Dick and Elaine Barber capsized on the Basswood River on their way to Argo Lake.

sleeping bags, and the emergency beacon. Dick, however, was trapped in the current. He was unable to swim or move in any direction more than a foot or two. Authorities later said it was possible that even then, less than a minute after tumbling into the water, Dick was suffering the immediate effects of hypothermia. In a 2013 interview with the *Pioneer Press* newspaper in St. Paul, Elaine said Dick "was screaming, 'I cannot move! I cannot move!' . . . It might have been hypothermia, I don't know. . . . It could have been the current."

Both Dick and Elaine were wearing their life jackets when they capsized and fell into the river. Elaine has questioned whether Dick had his personal floatation device properly secured, the jacket possibly being unzipped. When his body was recovered four days later, Dick's life jacket was nowhere to be found.

After watching her husband go under the water and never return, Elaine used the couple's emergency beacon to signal for help. By then it was getting dark, so she set up their tent on the banks of the Basswood River. She spent a mostly sleepless night knowing that her husband's body was churning in the swollen river, possibly less than a hundred yards from where she made camp on the rocky shoreline. The day all of this occurred, June 2, was Dick and Elaine's wedding anniversary.

When a reporter from CBS in Minneapolis asked Elaine less than a week after the incident what advice she has for anyone who loves the outdoors, she focused on situational awareness and carrying an emergency beacon. "Get prepared for the events that you don't think are going to happen, and if you go in, have a safety device with you," she said.

When Harold Hanson turned seventy-eight, he wanted to reach the top of Minnesota. In October 2021 he traveled to the Boundary Waters and accomplished this very feat. Hanson, along with his grandson, drove from his home in Ramsey, Minnesota, to climb Eagle Mountain, the state's highest peak. Eagle Mountain sits inside the wilderness line of the BWCA. The main trailhead is about twenty miles from Grand Marais. At 2,301 feet above sea level, reaching the top of Eagle Mountain is a far cry from summiting mountains in places like Colorado, Washington, or Oregon, but it's a popular destination for spirited hikers in the Upper Midwest nonetheless.

Though not for reasons Hanson enjoyed, the day of his hike to the top of Minnesota, October 10, ended up being historic. A tornado ripped through the Boundary Waters that afternoon. It was a serious tornado too, reaching an EF2 rating on the Enhanced Fujita intensity scale, meaning its wind speeds hovered around 120 miles per hour. After swooping over Eagle Mountain, the tornado touched down just north of the Gunflint Trail near East Bearskin Lake. From there it continued charging north before lifting in Ontario near Mountain Lake, a spectacular body of water that straddles the international border. The US side of Mountain Lake sits in the BWCA. The storm was most intense near Alder and Clearwater Lakes, just south of Mountain Lake, where massive pine trees broke with the ease of human hands snapping toothpicks. According to the National Weather Service, it was the first tornado ever recorded in the Boundary Waters in October. The event took down so many trees in the wilderness area that weather satellites captured images of a "tornado scar" just days later.

I paddled through the blowdown area in May 2022. The carnage was eerie. At one campsite on a north-facing peninsula on

Alder Lake, it looked as though a bomb had been dropped from above. Trees were lying on their sides, either flat on the ground or crisscrossed like a field of mixed-up letters. Exposed roots from fallen trees dotted the landscape. The woods seemed particularly uninviting. Yet the pure force of the storm was captivating. *A tornado rolled through here,* I thought from the safety of the Kevlar canoe, looking toward shore.

Though Hanson was in the Boundary Waters at the time, he never saw the tornado. Eagle Mountain is about thirty miles from Alder Lake. But Hanson also didn't know about the tornado because he was flat on his back on a stretcher having a heart attack.

"It was a historic day for me and for Minnesota, it turns out," Hanson told me in October 2022.

Before the storm and subsequent tornado rolled in, Hanson and his nineteen-year-old grandson safely reached the top of Eagle Mountain. The time was approximately 2:30 PM. The tornado would not officially touch down for another four hours. After taking in the summit and its views of the Misquah Hills, including numerous lakes scattered across the BWCA, the duo began their descent. It was close to 2:50 PM. Less than a mile from the summit, Hanson started to feel strange. His right leg went limp. Internally, his body felt very cold, as though he'd been swimming in Lake Superior. Despite the energy and natural high that often comes from summiting a mountain, he had a deep desire to lie down, which he did. A young man and woman Hanson had talked with on the summit were also descending from Eagle Mountain. They saw Hanson on the trail and ran up to assess the situation. "They asked me to smile, and I did, sort of," Hanson said. "I could move my whole mouth, so we knew it likely wasn't a stroke." It was obvious Hanson would need help getting off the mountain. The young woman continued down the trail to see if she could get cell service. She did, about a half mile from where Hanson was located. A 911 call reporting a seventy-year-old man having a heart attack came in to the Cook County Law Enforcement Center just before 3 PM, according to a summary sent to the media following the incident. Cook County Search and Rescue volunteers, Lutsen first responders, and other emergency personnel were at the Eagle Mountain trailhead thirty-five minutes later.

The Eagle Mountain Trail is lined with birch and conifers. Periodically, exposed cedar roots bulge from the earth along the trail. Over the years, trail volunteers and the Forest Service installed narrow stretches of boardwalk that allow hikers to travel over swamps and standing water. Most of the water comes from small creeks plugged by beaver dams. Some people jog on the trail, but most undertake a casual stroll as they make their way to the top of Minnesota. The emergency responders, in their quest to reach Hanson, had to carefully navigate the winding trail. They found him and the others at 4:25 PM. As they arrived, dark clouds rolled in overhead. Time was of the essence, primarily because Hanson was suffering from what appeared to be a heart attack. The crew worked quickly. As it started to rain, Hanson felt straps coming across his body. He recalls being placed on a stretcher "just as the heavy rain and high winds started." There were no wheels on the stretcher. The emergency responders would have to carry him out. Given the conditions and the terrain, and the fact they were carrying an elderly male in physical distress down a hiking trail on a stretcher, the miles-long descent back to the ambulance was slow. The weather grew worse. At 5:41 PM, the rescuers had to stop. They took shelter under a large spruce as the rain turned to hail. Golf ball–sized hailstones fell from a thunderous sky. Dispatch relayed a message over the communication radio that they needed to be ready for a tornado. At 5:44 PM a tornado warning was issued.

"What are the odds? They happen to be responding to a search and rescue on that day at that time, in that area, and we have a tornado touch down," Cook County sheriff Pat Eliasen told me several months after the incident. "I mean, what are the odds of that? That's just astronomical. They had to just hunker down, and it's like, *You know, hopefully we don't die out here.* I even thought about that the next day. You know, we've had one tornado touch down in Cook County in the last fifty years. And that had to be that day."

As the crew and others hid under the tree to marginally escape the pounding hail and strong wind, Hanson remembers leaning over the side of the stretcher and vomiting. "I was so cold," he said. "It actually felt kind of good to throw up." Hanson was immobile and freezing as the hail dropped around them. After several minutes, the storm eased as it charged toward the Gunflint Trail and Alder Lake, where it eventually morphed into an EF2 tornado.

As the storm moved north, the team picked up Hanson on the stretcher and continued down Eagle Mountain. They arrived at the trailhead and parking lot at 7:29 PM. The North Shore Health ambulance, Cook County Search and Rescue, Lutsen and Grand Marais first responders, and Cook County Sheriff's Office deputies all took part in the emergency call. In a public statement following the storm and the evacuation of Hanson from Eagle Mountain, Eliasen said the responders "deserve much respect for the job they perform under some very dangerous conditions. I cannot express enough gratitude for these folks and the sacrifices they make." For his part, Hanson told me he was "forever grateful" for the "tremendous work those people did" in getting him safely down the mountain.

Hanson was taken by Cook County/North Shore Health ambulance directly to St. Luke's Hospital in Duluth. He spent several days there, including "two days just trying to get warm," he said. The medical staff at St. Luke's put a stent in his heart, and he made a full recovery. By the time we touched base a year later, he was already talking about a desire to return to the Boundary Waters.

"It's right up there with my favorite places on this planet," he said.

Hanson, who has white hair, a thick Minnesota accent, and the calm demeanor often exhibited by midwesterners of Scandinavian descent, has spent most of his life fascinated by the Boundary Waters. He and his wife spent their honeymoon in Grand Marais following their wedding in Ely on October 2, 1965. Most of Hanson's adult life involved making at least one trip to the Boundary Waters each year. Despite suffering a heart attack on a hiking trail and being carried out on a stretcher in a tornado, Hanson said the BWCA remains one of his most cherished locations.

"It's a wild place, and that was a big adventure," he said. "But that's part of what makes the place so unique. It is a wild place. That's why we go."

IV

Across Superior National Forest, most search and rescue operations unfold in a calculated manner. Someone gets lost or injured or finds themselves in a precarious situation they can't get out of and needs professional assistance. The person in distress either pushes a button on an emergency beacon, uses their cell phone to call for help, or asks someone who happens to find them to go and get help. Cook, Lake, and St. Louis Counties in northeastern Minnesota all have their own version of a search and rescue squad, with the St. Louis County Rescue Squad that Rick Slatten is on being by far the largest.

The initial focus of any search and rescue operation in the Boundary Waters is to locate, access, stabilize, and transport individuals in distress. The scenarios could include a canoeist who capsizes and is now stuck on an island without any gear, a person who severely sprains their ankle on a portage trail, someone who had a heart attack, or someone who is suffering from hypothermia. In 2021 the St. Louis County Rescue Squad responded to nearly five hundred calls, Slatten said—an average of more than one call each day of the year. Their coverage area is massive, some seven thousand square miles, an area roughly the size of

New Jersey. Each year they respond to calls spread across the abundant woods and on the waters of northeastern Minnesota, from the shores of Lake Superior to mine pits on the Iron Range. Narrowing the scope to the BWCA, however, between May 15 and October 1 of 2021, they responded to a dozen calls specifically inside the most-visited wilderness in the nation. In 2020, during the first year of the pandemic and the subsequent surge of outdoor activity across the nation, the rescue squad responded to a record twenty-six calls in the BWCA. In 2019 the St. Louis County Rescue Squad responded to eighteen calls inside the BWCA, though several of those were for accidental activations of an emergency beacon.

After someone makes their distress call or word reaches the authorities that help is needed in the Boundary Waters, the search and rescue operation is initiated. The team gathers at a staging location, either one of their facilities or another similar base of operations. If it makes logistical sense, some responders will join directly at the trailhead or entry point where the team will enter the wilderness to find the person in distress. The first objective is to find the person. If someone triggers their emergency beacon and does not move, this part of the situation is fairly easy to handle. Much like the term states, the scenario would be a rescue, as opposed to a search. Another example is if the person calls from their cell phone and says they are at a particular campsite on a particular lake: again, the "Where is this person?" part of the equation is essentially eliminated.

If the search and rescue team does not know exactly where the distressed party is, its first objective is to establish a search area. The search area is "an amoeba called the 'max containment zone,'" Slatten said. The max containment zone can be—and often is—changed based on the discovery of new data, Slatten points out. An initial phase in helping to set up this zone is to determine where the missing person was last seen, which is known in the search and rescue industry as a PLS, or point last seen. This could be an outfitter where the person rented a canoe or a parking lot near a trailhead along places like the Echo Trail or Gunflint Trail.

The next phase is to determine if an article of clothing or some other item associated with the person they are looking for has been found along a trail. This point then becomes what people in the search and rescue industry appropriately title the "last known position." An example would be Skelton's clothing and other possessions that were found near the Angleworm Trail. The items Skelton dropped on the trail established the max containment zone. Slatten explained all of this to me at the St. Louis County Rescue Squad headquarters near Duluth. We reviewed large maps and went over specific cases, discussing the various methods the search team uses in the field. Slatten pointed on the map to Whisky Jack Lake, showing me where the searches took place. "We looked here, here, and all over this area here," he said, gesturing toward the western shoreline of the BWCA lake.

Slatten and the St. Louis County Rescue Squad typically use a scientific analysis process involving mathematical equations to determine the probability of where someone is likely to be. They also use something known as a "missing person behavioral profile" to find who they are looking for. These tables break down situations when people with similar traits were engaged in a comparable activity, went missing or were in distress, and were then rescued. The scenarios could occur in the Boundary Waters or in other areas with dense forest, rivers, and lakes. In other words, Slatten tells me, when many people think about what a search and rescue operation involves, they typically don't understand how calculated the process is. "People tend to think we just walk through the woods, hoping to find somebody, or that maybe we'll trip over a body and say, 'Hey! Over here!' It doesn't work like that," he said. "The public perception of a search is largely getting a group of people shoulder to shoulder and moving through the woods. Searching is way more scientific than that. We employ human trackers, canines, drones, helicopter and fixed-wing aircraft, sound searching, trail running, and a ton of investigation."

The process of finding someone who is lost in the woods is urgent, though not chaotic. Michael Valentini is a member of the Gunflint Trail Fire Department. He responds to assorted emergency situations on the east side of the BWCA. In September 2018 Valentini and others from the Cook County Sheriff's Department, Cook County Search and Rescue, and the Gunflint Trail Volunteer Fire Department received word of a missing hiker. Bob Klaver, a professor from Iowa State University, had been traversing the Border Route Trail, a rugged pathway that runs across the northeastern side of the wilderness. Klaver started his trek September 1 on the Daniels Lake spur trail off of Clearwater Road. After backpacking for two days along the Border Route, he followed a rough section of trail to a campsite at Partridge Lake. There Klaver's canister of bear spray was accidentally deployed when it caught on a tree branch. The spray covered Klaver's torso and got in his eyes, temporarily blinding him for several hours.

Klaver opted to remain on the shores of Partridge Lake and wait for a search and rescue team to find him rather than risk becoming lost in the dense forest surrounding the lake. He was not badly injured, as the bear spray only temporarily affected his vision. Other than that, he was essentially unscathed. However, he'd lost

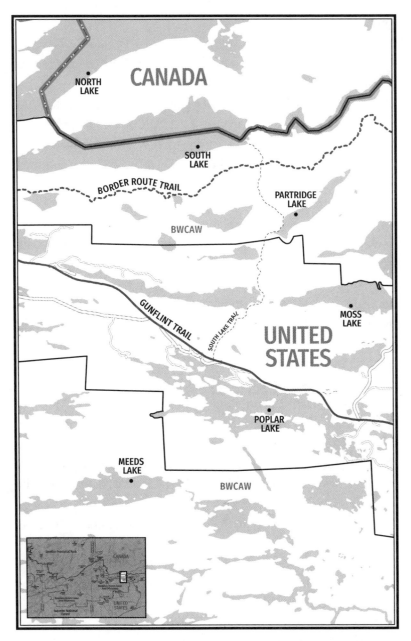

While hiking the Border Route Trail, Bob Klaver awaited rescue at
Partridge Lake.

the trail, and he didn't want to become completely bewildered in the surrounding dense forest. Rather than risk making a bad situation worse, he more or less stopped moving. On the first night he spent on the shores of Partridge, Klaver slept under a tarp. On the second day, he pitched his tent, taking comfort inside the shelter. "I was glad I did," Klaver said. "It rained most of that day and night."

After friends in Iowa notified local law enforcement that Klaver was missing, a floatplane found him on the afternoon of September 5. The pilot spotted Klaver largely because the distressed hiker was waving a red sleeping pad. The people on the plane were not in fact actively looking for Klaver. The passengers included a team of biologists involved in a wolf study in northeastern Minnesota, Klaver said. In reality, the people in the aircraft more or less happened upon Klaver, taking note of him because he was frantically waving the red sleeping pad.

In statements sent to Grand Marais media, Valentini said there are two important lessons to take away from the incident. "The expertise and efficiency of law enforcement, dispatch, search and rescue, the USFS and the fire department working hand in hand made this a well-coordinated recovery. But make no mistake; it was the levelheaded thinking on Bob Klaver's part that had the most to do with the success."

I spoke with Klaver in 2018 and again in 2022 about his experience. He told me that, while he is grateful for the responding agencies' efforts, he is "still a little bit embarrassed about the whole thing." Still, Klaver believes he did the right thing by staying put on Partridge Lake and waiting for rescue. The fact that the paved Gunflint Trail was about two and a half miles away and that he could have pressed on, finding the South Lake Trail and essentially ending up at Rockwood Lodge, his ultimate destination before returning to Iowa, did not deter Klaver from his reasoning. Disoriented after the incident with the bear spray and confused as to his exact location on Partridge Lake, Klaver did not want to make the situation any worse. So he dropped everything and basically sat down, waiting for someone to come find him.

Valentini said this was the right choice for several reasons. "First he didn't panic. He calmly assessed his situation. Rather than keep walking blindly, he made his way to the shore of a lake, set up a camp in a site that would be visible to searchers on water and air. Then he waited for help to come his way. He had plenty of firewood to keep a campfire going and foliage to throw on the fire to create a smoke signal. He was fully aware that when he didn't return on time that help would be coming his way."

After Klaver was hauled out of the BWCA via a floatplane, he was flown to a large dock at Hungry Jack Lake. He went inside for a cheeseburger. About an hour later, he drove back to Iowa. It was a story that made the local news, though perhaps some wondered why Klaver didn't just walk out under his own power. As it goes with locating missing people or getting lost in the woods, there isn't always a clear and defined solution to a problem. In this instance, Klaver said when he spoke with US Forest Service officials shortly after the incident, they told him he did everything right.

The search and rescue teams that work in and around the Boundary Waters are tight-knit organizations primarily made up of trained volunteers. They deploy at the request of other agencies, such as the Cook County Sheriff's Office in Grand Marais or local law enforcement in Ely. The agencies are funded by in-kind donations, federal dollars, and a levy as allocated by the county sheriff's department. Slatten said the "only money we can write checks against, and what really keeps the search and rescue squad going" are public donations. The St. Louis County Rescue Squad near Duluth does a blanket mailing to about 110,000 addresses throughout the massive county.

"There's a letter and a window sticker and we ask them for money," he said of the requests for community support.

The second source of funding for the three counties that provide assistance in the Boundary Waters comes from the state's boat and water safety grant program. The Minnesota Department of Natural Resources allocates these dollars "to assist counties through their sheriffs' offices in funding boating safety equipment and aids to navigation to help carry out their legislatively-mandated boating safety duties. The goal: to reduce deaths, injuries and property damage on state waters." The money for these grants comes from fishing license sales and boating registration costs for individual anglers and people who recreate on various watercraft in Minnesota. Finally, local jurisdictions indicate how much financial support they are willing to provide on an annual basis. In the much less populated Cook County, Sheriff Pat Eliasen said he works hard every year to get the Gunflint Trail and other search and rescue teams some level of financial support.

Slatten said it costs more than $300,000 a year to run the St. Louis County Rescue Squad. "In exchange for that," he's quick to point out, "the public gets about $3 million in free labor. So we think we're a pretty good bargain."

In terms of boots on the ground, search and rescue operations near the BWCA can take many forms: ground searches, water rescues via canoe or motorized boat, K9 search and rescue, flood and swift water rescue, vertical rescue, and aerial searches. The type of operation varies depending on if the campsite or lake is entirely within the BWCA, as well as on the weather, available assets, and a variety of circumstances dictated by the incident, Slatten added.

Slatten recalled a rescue from 2015 that illustrates the complexities of responding to critical situations in the BWCA. On a warm day in June, Slatten said, "a canoe capsized in some white water, and because of the hydraulics of the water, the canoe was pressing a teenager into a rock and drowning him." The teen was a member of the Boy Scouts on a trip to the Boundary Waters. Slatten said a scoutmaster did his best to keep the young man safe until search and rescue officials could arrive. "He held the boy's head above water for two hours," Slatten said, adding that for the rescue to happen, the St. Louis County Rescue Squad built a hauling system with rope gear to pull the canoe off the rock. Once the boy was freed from the pressure of the water and the canoe that was pinned to the rock, "we could get him out of there," Slatten said.

Slatten offers another example of a successful search and rescue operation involving two experienced BWCA paddlers who spent six days lost in the wilderness. He said the rescue of Minnesotans Chuck Kelly and Pamela Scaia is "textbook" in how a Boundary Waters search and rescue mission can work to perfection.

Kelly and Scaia's paddling trip near Ely took place in late May 2017. The excursion was going well until the duo took a wrong turn near Oyster Lake. On their ninth day out they paddled up a swollen creek, mistaking it for a tributary that would lead them from the Oyster River to the Nina Moose River, Scaia told me in 2022. The creek became impenetrable after many hours of strenuous travel. At a certain point, Scaia knew they'd gone too far and that backtracking would be nearly impossible. They stopped moving, set up camp, and decided to wait. Their planned exit was May 29. Three days later, on June 1, Scaia's daughter called 911.

"Mom didn't show up for work," Slatten said. "So that's what touches this off."

Slatten said the search for Kelly and Scaia covered air, land, and water, and in addition to the rescue squad, the search involved the US Forest Service, Minnesota State Patrol, National Guard, and officials from the Minnesota Department of Natural Resources. The communication between the agencies was phenomenal, Slatten said. Crews paddled from Moose Lake to Lac La Croix looking for Kelly, who was sixty-six at the time, and Scaia, who was sixty-five. Aerial searches were underway as well, which is how the search and rescue team ultimately found the duo camped on the edge of a swamp.

I spoke with Scaia in August 2022 about her experience being rescued in the Boundary Waters. An animated and spirited individual, she told me, "Chuck and I were very experienced in the woods. And we had quality gear, we had maps, we had a compass, and because we got impatient, because we were stubborn, we ended up getting lost." As they strayed from the Oyster River, Scaia said, they "went farther and deeper into the swamp and the bogs."

"It was my fault that we kept pushing, I guess," Scaia told me. "Because after you've carried your damn kayak, or your damn canoe, up a sort of waterfall, things change. I did not want to go back. I kept saying, 'Look, the next lake has got to be up there. It's got to be around the next turn. It's over the next pile of rocks.' At one point, we were carrying the canoe through woods, through thick woods. That's when I cried."

In the 2008 book *Lost Person Behavior: A Search and Rescue Guide on Where to Look—for Land, Air and Water*, author Robert Koester explains that often people get lost in the woods because of what they expect to find around the next curve in the trail or bend in the river. Slatten agrees, noting that pushing forward when you're lost usually leads to bad situations. "The reason people are extremely reluctant to turn around, and usually it is a male hiker or canoeist, is they always believe that the post, the signpost, or the junction that's going to solve all their problems is just around the next bend."

By the time rescue crews reached Kelly and Scaia—in a Black Hawk helicopter that came from the Army National Guard, no less—they had spent almost two weeks in the BWCA. During their final days, they were consuming about three hundred calories a day, most of that coming from the one pack of instant oatmeal they allowed themselves to eat. During the time when she was considered lost in the Boundary Waters, Scaia said she never feared for her life. "Chuck and I, we're great travel companions. He was in the army in Alaska. He's a tough guy. If anything, I was the crybaby. We were there for twelve days, and had food for nine days. But we had water and we kept a fire. And we stayed dry. We had a tent and we stayed warm. So, you know, we could have lasted for a long time. I would have killed my kids if they didn't look for me, though."

Scaia is far from a rugged BWCA camper. She voluntarily told me she weighs 112 pounds. She enjoys outdoor recreation, but she also enjoys the bright lights of a city. There were times, she admits, when she thought about how her kids would deal with her death if she didn't make it out of the Boundary Waters alive. That's why an airplane flying close to the ground on their final night in the woods was among the most magical sounds she'd ever heard. Kelly and Scaia assumed the plane flying overhead saw them as they shined their flashlight toward the night sky. What caught Scaia off guard was how soon after the plane flew over that another aircraft, this time a helicopter, returned to the scene. "We had seen some other planes flying over in the previous days. But this time, we heard one come closer, and Chuck ran out and was signaling him with his light. And then they tip their wings to tell us that they had seen us. And we said, 'Okay, wonderful; they'll come for us in the morning.' But within an hour, this guy looking like a cyborg from *Star Wars* comes walking through the woods. They had dropped him down. And he's wearing night goggles and everything. I recall his helmet and night goggles so clearly. And he comes walking through the woods and said, 'No, we're getting you out of here now.'"

Slatten recalls this rescue as being so good because of excellent communication among numerous responding agencies. Furthermore, the process of "investigate, contain, and search was spot-on." Slatten said the dimensions of where Scaia and Kelly could have potentially been located was spread across a "huge area" in the BWCA. Yet certain data said "look here. And that's where they were," Slatten explained.

"It was a phenomenal search, one of the best I've been on," he told a group of reporters shortly after the experience. "We truly saved lives that night. What we did mattered."

V

Jordan Grider's skull is still out there. At least whatever's left of it. The wolves took the rest.

Grider traveled more than fourteen hundred miles from New Mexico to Minnesota in October 2018 to get to the BWCA. He died alone in the wilderness a few days later. Authorities believe his death was an accident. A mistake swinging an ax is one theory. An accidental firing of his handgun is another. Accident or not, when law enforcement found Grider's final campsite, blood and chaos stood out above everything else. His final moments on earth were not peaceful.

Grider's skull is believed to be still out there because of the simple fact that it's never been found. As authorities searched the area of his final campsite, some of Grider's bones were discovered. Most were not. Wildlife officials believe animals carried away, chewed on, and perhaps ate most of the bones. These animals range from large carnivores like bears and wolves to small rodents such as mice. Or perhaps the skeletal remains of his head simply sank into the gluey earth. The forest floor is soft near the beaver pond where the young man from New Mexico made his last camp. After a number of extensive searches, only a dozen of Grider's bones were found, near where law enforcement officials

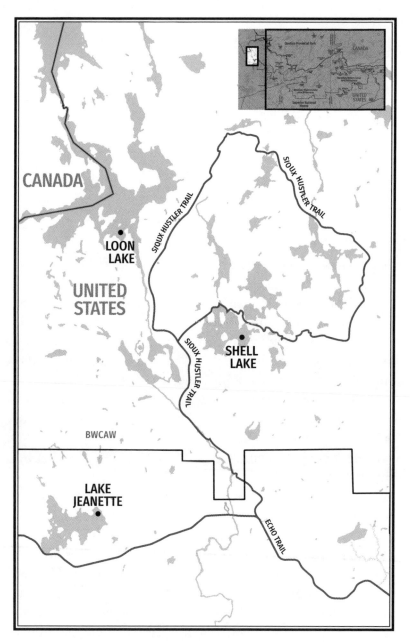

Jordan Grider's campsite was near the Sioux Hustler Trail.

located Grider's hammock and sleeping bag hanging between two poplar trees. Both the hammock and the sleeping bag were covered in blood. The hammock hung not far from the Sioux Hustler Trail, a hiking path that meanders across the BWCA. Grider was twenty-nine years old when he died.

I traveled to New Mexico the week after Thanksgiving in 2021 to learn what brought Grider from the arid desert to the far reaches of northeastern Minnesota. My journey took me to Moriarty, New Mexico, Grider's hometown, about an hour east of Albuquerque. The community proudly brands itself as "The Crossroads of Opportunity," recognizing the many highways and interstates crisscrossing near town, including the iconic Route 66. The town's population hovers near two thousand souls, many of them deeply religious and poor. Michael Moriarty, for whom the town is named, brought his family from Iowa to New Mexico in 1887 to "avoid the cold winters" of the Midwest, according to a summary shared inside the town's community center.

Minnesota—known for its long, brutal winters—might as well be the North Pole by comparison. Northwest winds ripping south from Canada are a near constant across the Boundary Waters each winter. Heavy snow piles on top of ice, and the ground locks with a deep freeze. When Grider left New Mexico and headed north, he knew little of the cold that was waiting for him. He'd never felt forty below zero, let alone made an attempt to camp and live in such extreme conditions.

"We wanted him to wait until spring," Jordan's mother, Rebecca, told me before I arrived. "We didn't like the idea of a winter in the woods in Minnesota. Nobody did, other than Jordan."

The Grider home in Moriarty has a blue metal roof atop the structure's stucco walls. White trim hangs snug around the windows and the front door. Scrubby pine and one-seed junipers dot the front yard. An empty lot across the street resembles something out of the old West. It's a scene where someone who looks and acts like Doc Holliday or Wyatt Earp might suddenly come riding up on horseback, and nobody would say much about it.

Jordan was the third born among the six Grider boys. The others are Joey, Jonathan, Jesse, Joshua, and James. Rebecca, his mother, was eighteen when Jordan entered the world. She never finished high school.

All of the Grider boys were homeschooled, something Jordan resented and never made peace with, his mother said. He was athletic and curious but never learned to read or write beyond an elementary-grade level. Jordan was dyslexic, but this learning disability was not diagnosed until he was twelve. Public health officials were essentially baffled at the severity of his dyslexia, Rebecca said. Over time, his learning disability and lack of education manifested in his unruly engagement with the world. The Mayo Clinic in Minnesota reports that when left untreated, dyslexia may lead to low self-esteem, behavioral problems, anxiety, aggression, and withdrawal from friends and family. For most of his life Grider suffered from many of these symptoms. Trouble with the law and a tendency to slip into the dark shadows of society, or to abandon it altogether, were manifestations of the turmoil that spun a web in his mind on a daily basis.

Talking about Jordan's death with his parents was challenging; his dad, Jason, broke down to tears multiple times throughout the course of the gray December afternoon when we met. "It's not easy losing a child," he choked out. As Jason wept in front of me that afternoon in the kitchen, his son's bones lay dormant in a cardboard box in a nearby room. Aside from the memories and the stories his parents shared with me, that was all that was left of Jordan Grider. He was a dozen bones in a box.

Before Grider arrived in Ely and the Boundary Waters, he'd never been to Minnesota. The only reference he had to the Boundary Waters came from the campfire he shared years before with others along the Appalachian Trail. Somebody told him it was as remote a place as one could hope to find in America, even more secluded than the strange backwoods of Kentucky. Appalachia and the rolling hills of eastern Kentucky were home for Grider from 2012 to 2017. Here he took to camping—indeed, living— in the woods near the small town of Manchester.

Located near the massive Daniel Boone National Forest, Clay County and nearby communities, including Manchester, London, and East Bernstadt, served as Jordan's hub for the bulk of his twenties. Grider essentially lived out of his truck when he arrived in Kentucky in 2012, though he kept his hammock hanging in the nearby woods, within eyesight of his vehicle. Grider chose to be homeless during this period, his mother said. He liked the nomadic lifestyle and being free from the burdens of rent, landlords, and utility bills arriving in the mail.

Much like Superior National Forest in Minnesota where the Boundary Waters is located, Daniel Boone National Forest is renowned for its natural beauty. Hardwood trees decorate the rugged landscape, and a series of reservoirs and flowing rivers sneaks between steep sandstone ridges. Despite the beauty of the woods and waters encompassing the region, in a 2014 article the *New York Times* described Clay County as being one of the poorest and worst places to live in the nation.

Jordan Grider kept his camp there. The same hammock authorities found soaked in blood in the Boundary Waters hung between two trees for about four of the five years Grider lived in Kentucky. The trees stood on land owned by a farmer named Durrell Rudolph. "Jordan was a nice kid; he didn't ask for much or do anything that gave us a reason to be worried about him living here," Rudolph told me in 2022 when I traveled to Kentucky.

I met Rudolph in pretty much the same way Jordan Grider did: I just showed up. Matthew Baxley, my frequent companion on trips to the BWCA and Quetico, and I traveled to Kentucky in August 2022 to learn more about where Grider spent years camping and isolating in the woods. Rudolph and his family are Mennonites, and the day I met Durrell he wore black rubber boots, black denim pants held up by black suspenders, and a white long-sleeve collared shirt with vertical translucent stripes. The shirt and pants were filthy. Atop his head sat a clean, yellow straw hat. We talked at length about Grider. "I heard of his passing," Rudolph said. "It was so sad."

Rudolph's voice is thick with a southern accent and the unique drawl of someone who has clearly spent a lot of time on a farm. The easy assumption could be that Rudolph is a hick living in the woods of Appalachia. The reality is that his kindness and generosity supersede the stereotypes. He welcomed Baxley and me onto his land in the same way he welcomed Grider: without judgment. "It's a slower way of life here for me and my family than maybe most people care for, but we do work for it, for everything we have. We feel quite blessed. Really, this is a pretty good place."

The patch of land where Grider made his camp in Kentucky is similar in many ways to the makeshift campsite he chose near the Sioux Hustler Trail on the edge of the Boundary Waters. The site in Kentucky was tucked away, surrounded by thick timber and brush, and probably not a place where most people would want to spend a lot of time. The shallow Goose Creek trickles near the spot where Grider kept his hammock. On the day I was there, Rudolph's beef cattle stood lazily in the shade on the other side of the creek, no more than twenty yards from Grider's former camp. "Jordan would bathe down there in the creek," Rudolph said. Empty bottles, tires, and other rubbish were scattered across the forest floor, possibly remnants of Grider's camp, or a combination of litter tossed from the nearby road.

Similar to New Mexico, southeastern Kentucky does not have anything that comes close to a Minnesota winter. The average temperature in winter is above freezing in Clay County, though it does snow on occasion. Any snow typically melts away within forty-eight hours. Nonetheless, Grider, about two years into his stay on the property near Goose Creek, set about constructing a makeshift shelter to supplement his hammock-and-tarp sleeping quarters, which more or less served as his home base of operations. The structure was rough, a tin roof and plywood walls, all of it held up by scrap two-by-fours from various Mennonite construction projects. Grider had cut a hole in the roof of the small structure and installed a barrel stove, essentially creating a small warming hut that could double as a sauna. "He would call it a bathhouse," Rudolph said. Eventually, however, a dead tree fell on the small building and destroyed it. Not long after, Grider departed the Bluegrass State.

Late October—when Grider first arrived in Minnesota—is a time of transition across Superior National Forest. Indeed, many things are changing within this massive swath of federal land during autumn. Tamarack trees are turning gold before their needles drop to the forest floor. Loons are restless, preparing to fly south before all the water becomes frozen and inhospitable. Even with the best gear money can buy, from canvas-wall tents with woodstoves to sleeping bags rated to twenty below zero

Fahrenheit, spending a winter in the BWCA requires dedicated planning, investment, and resources. Grider didn't have the best gear money could buy. In fact, he had terrible gear. He didn't have much of a plan either. He had some bags of rice, a few bags of dried beans, and some basic knowledge of survival. More important, he was entirely unfamiliar with the landscape. The area where he chose to camp offered little in the way of sustainability and harvest. There were no fish in the little beaver pond near his camp, and even if there were, once the pond froze, he'd have no means to find them. He did not have an auger to drill through the ice. Once winter arrived, it's possible, likely even, that Grider would have packed up and gone home. He died before the cold had a chance to grip his intentions and squeeze out his resolve. Though he wanted to spend the entire winter in the BWCA, he presumably died just a few days after he arrived in Minnesota.

Despite the uncertainty of exactly how he died, most people— from law enforcement to Grider's family members—agree his body was eaten by wolves. On occasion, wolves will go beyond chewing or crushing whatever it is they are eating and will, in fact, eat bones—for calcium and other minerals. Ribs are a favorite, along with other small bones. Over a cup of coffee one afternoon, Seth Moore, a wildlife biologist who works near the BWCA, told me everything I'd ever need to know about the feeding habits of wolves. Moore is the director of biology and environment for the Grand Portage Band of Lake Superior Chippewa in northeastern Minnesota. He said that wolves typically eat almost everything of whatever it is they're consuming. They love deer and young moose, but anything with flesh and blood will suffice. "They'll eat skin; they'll eat hair; they'll chew through the bones. You can find teeth and hooves in wolf scat," Moore explained.

Moore has spent more than a decade studying wolves on the edge of the Boundary Waters and Lake Superior, including a massive undertaking with the federal government to transfer wolves from the Minnesota and Ontario mainland to Isle Royale National Park. Moore said wolves have an amazing ability to carry things—perhaps even a human skull—long distances. "We've had wolves prey on moose, for example. Sometimes they'll grab the [GPS tracking] collar, not biological material at all, and they'll just carry the collar for a mile and drop it. Luckily, our [tracking] collars have GPS units so we can find them. But it's not associated with the moose carcass at all. They'll do the same thing with pelvises. They'll do the same thing with heads. You know, sometimes we'll find moose heads very far away from where the rest of the bones in the carcass was. For a human skull, I suspect they probably just hauled it off."

When recovering dead bodies from the Boundary Waters, particularly in a situation like Jordan Grider's, where he was in the woods for months before his remains were discovered, search and rescue squads understand they might not find the body in one place. Rick Slatten said he was not the least bit confused when the St. Louis County Rescue Squad and other agencies found some of Grider's bones but not his skull. "It's fairly common not to find the skull in a case like this. It's frequently taken by scavengers, let's put it that way," Slatten said.

Dead people tend to rot rather quickly: Slatten tells me this somewhat abruptly, changing the subject from what we've been discussing. Decaying typically starts within five minutes after a person dies, Slatten says, and "scent detectable to the human remains detection dogs begins to appear within minutes of death." Slatten is prone to talk about graphic imagery and death in the way most people might mention the weather. Blood, rotting flesh, pain—all of this is the world Slatten might enter on any given day. Decades of experience in the field have desensitized him to what most people gingerly discuss. We're all going to die, Slatten understands; it's just a matter of how messy it will be and what steps it will take to move the body to the county coroner's office.

Slatten and I spent close to an hour one cold afternoon in December 2021 talking about Grider's death. It was the fifth time I'd reached out to Slatten seeking information about people who have died, been injured, or gone missing in the Boundary Waters region. As usual, he was forthcoming and brutally honest. Basically, Slatten says, the Grider case was a search operation where the team went in looking for human remains. The word "rescue" was not part of the equation. The team brought human remains detection dogs (commonly referred to as cadaver dogs) to assist with the mission, and there was nothing unique or extraordinary about the situation from a tactical standpoint, Slatten explains. When I ask him about all the attention Grider's death garnered on the internet, on various Boundary Waters blogs and discussions forums, Slatten essentially shrugs his shoulders.

Pressing harder, I tell him that many of the commenters in these online threads discuss the wolves. Any media coverage about Grider's death also made sure to mention the wolves, typically in the headline. My own line of questioning, we both observe, focuses on when and how the pack of wolves in the Boundary Waters came to eat Jordan Grider. After a few more exchanges, Slatten settles on this: Wolves are not the biggest threat to humans in the wilderness. It's the people themselves. Forget everything about the wolves in this case, Slatten says. The biggest threat to somebody on their trip to the Boundary Waters is the person themselves. I ask him to repeat the statement.

"The biggest threat to somebody on their trip to the wilderness is themselves," he says. "The wolf stuff, that's just a lot of Hollywood media. The big bad wolf, all that. I can't recall any search or rescue situations, in my experience, where predators have been involved, at least not while the person was still alive. You know, the wolves didn't do it. The bears didn't do it. The windigo didn't do it. When we have calls from the Boundary Waters, it usually comes back to either simple forces of nature or choices the individual made while they were out there."

As I spoke with people about Jordan Grider—from casual canoeists who recreate in the Boundary Waters to law enforcement and emergency responders in Grand Marais and Duluth—they often compared him to one specific individual: Chris McCandless. Made famous by author Jon Krakauer in his book *Into the Wild* and a subsequent Sean Penn film by the same name, McCandless inspired an ideology built upon breaking free from society and roaming the United States with reckless abandon. Traveling under the name Alexander Supertramp, McCandless gave up his worldly possessions not long after graduating from college in 1990. Though he was raised in a wealthy family on the Eastern Seaboard, McCandless wrote extensively in his journal about what he viewed as the falsehoods of the American dream. In the McCandless narrative, money is bad, possessions are traps, humans are meant to be free spirits, and so on. After wandering the country for about two years, McCandless eventually hitchhiked to Alaska. The notion of going north appealed to him. In Alaska he found his way to a secluded though fairly accessible patch of wilderness near the Sushana River. There, he took shelter in an abandoned bus. Though the exact details of his death remain uncertain, it appears McCandless died of starvation and possibly poisoning after consuming toxic plants he found growing near the bus. His body was found decomposing in the bus by someone hunting for moose several months after McCandless entered the wilds of Alaska.

The obvious parallels are that both McCandless and Grider were white men in their twenties who took issue with the status quo. They wore beards on their faces and enjoyed being nomads. Their journeys were largely about themselves, certainly not about protecting the environment or some type of championing for the earth. They each had issues with their fathers and wanted to break from capitalism's confinement. There are many thousands like them, young men who think capitalism is the root of all the woes plaguing society. After grumbling through the cycle, most people of a similar mindset settle for doing things like baking bread in a wood-fired oven and selling it at a local farmers' market. Others keep at it. Some, like McCandless and Grider, die in the woods, and their stories end up on a bookshelf. Regardless of how famous these young men have become, their lives and subsequent deaths do not impress Slatten, the chiseled woodsman from the St. Louis County Rescue Squad.

"Chris McCandless, I mean, he had a movie made about him, but he was an idiot," Slatten told me in December 2021. "He went in thoroughly unprepared. And 'Mr. Blue Bird on my shoulder,' the Walt Disney approach to nature, you know, all that crap. The thing is, nature can be very giving, and it can be very taking away. Nature is the ultimate creator. And it's the ultimate destroyer. And, yeah, this Walt Disney approach that I can go in and find harmony with the universe, it's just hogwash."

Slatten says that no matter how Grider died, be it an accident with his ax or his gun or while shaving with a sharp knife, when he arrived in the Boundary Waters he was not equipped to spend a winter in northern Minnesota. "Grider was unprepared for what he was getting himself into. When you think about it, it's not much different from McCandless and the bus. Grider, he's on an old forest road. If the Forest Service hadn't dynamited the bridge, you could drive on it today. But the feds designated this a wilderness. But I'm telling you, this thing was a freeway back in the logging days. And he's not that far in the woods. I mean, as the crow flies, he's less than a mile from a pretty main road. He's forty-five hundred feet in the woods from the Echo Trail. And that's not very remote when it comes to the Boundary Waters and this huge area we cover." Similarly, McCandless and the bus he found were not far from an accessible road. Although McCandless was convinced that high water trapped him from crossing the Teklanika River when he wanted to leave the wilderness, in reality he was a short distance from a steel cable that stretched across the river and included a bucket and pulley system that would have ushered him to safety.

I first met Slatten on his turf, inside the St. Louis Rescue Squad headquarters off Highway 53 on the outskirts of Duluth. For this conversation, the one about Grider's death and his missing skull, I was in Grand Marais. Slatten told me that cell phone reception remains spotty across most of the BWCA, though it is increasing. However, if someone suffers a serious injury in the Boundary Waters, death is a necessary talking point for search and rescue squads to consider. How long before this person dies? It's something Slatten and others involved with search and rescue operations in and around the BWCA have to think about each time a distress call comes in.

After a brief hiatus—and at my prompting, to be fair—Slatten and I are once again talking about Grider's skull. Slatten says the head of a dead animal—in this case, a dead human—is easily detached and offers a food source for predators. The head can be moved to another location and then fed upon. Some of this we've already discussed, but Slatten talks about it as though we just discovered this fact. He's enthusiastic about the science, about the truth of the natural world. I listen patiently and attentively as he tells me that a wolf could easily have carried Grider's head a significant distance away from the spot where his bones were later discovered. That's why the skull is likely to never be found.

Grider's skull is now a part of the Boundary Waters.

PART III

Fire and Ice

I

Greg Welch was planning to go fishing from his kayak when hell rolled in.

The experience was a sensory overload. First he smelled the fire; then he heard it. Eventually he saw flames. And they were moving. Fast. Of all the clues that a wildfire was charging toward his camp in the BWCA, the sound gripped him the hardest.

"It started out as just a couple of twigs breaking off in the distance, in the woods," he said. "And then it got louder. Instead of tree limbs snapping, it sounded more like trees breaking and coming down in loud crashes. The closer it got, the more it sounded like you were standing in between a couple of freight trains that were coming by at a hundred miles an hour."

The day before, the US Forest Service employee at the ranger station in Tofte, Minnesota, had told Greg and his wife, Julie, about something called "the Pagami Creek Fire." The fire was a good distance, indeed miles away, from their entry point on Kawishiwi Lake. Besides, according to the person handing over their permit, the fire—sparked by a lightning strike—was small and more or less stagnant.

When Greg and Julie reached their entry point, it was a picturesque fall day in the Boundary Waters. The surface of the lake was calm. The temperature held steady at nearly seventy degrees for most of the afternoon as they paddled to Kawasachong Lake. After two portages and a modest amount of paddling, they selected a campsite on the western side of the lake.

This was the couple's seventeenth consecutive year making a trip from their home in Michigan to the Boundary Waters. Though they typically travel across the BWCA in a tandem canoe, on this particular trip they had separate kayaks. On day two, after a leisurely morning and early afternoon in camp, Greg decided it was time to go fishing. It was September 12, 2011.

Just before he left to chase some fish, Greg and Julie noticed the air start to change colors. It was getting later in the afternoon, around 4 PM, and everything, from the view across the lake to the thick stand of trees behind their tent, seemed to take on a touch of gray. Greg, a photojournalist who also owns a company that builds docks for cabin owners, took a photo of the darkening sky to the west. He pulled up the image on the camera screen and noticed orange streaks embedded within what appeared to be clouds. Around this time, Greg and Julie started to hear the sound of branches breaking in the dense forest behind them. The couple began feeling anxious, so Greg climbed down the steep, twenty-five-foot embankment from their campsite above the lake. He got in his kayak and paddled toward a spot where the Kawishiwi River meets the lake. This position opened his view to the north. All he saw was fire. A literal wall of flame was moving toward the lake.

Greg frantically paddled back to camp. Even before he arrived, Julie knew the situation was getting worse. She proactively began packing their gear into waterproof dry bags. The tension built with each decision. *What should we pack? Where are we going? Is our campsite about to burn up?* Communication became almost impossible as the fire moved closer.

"Talking to each other was actually difficult to do because there was so much noise," Greg said. "It was very windy, very wavy on the lake. It was just a lot of chaos."

Large, hot embers began flying through the air all over their camp. The smoke was now so thick it was difficult to see even a few feet in any direction. Both Greg and Julie grabbed a dry bag and bolted. They fled the campsite and made it to their kayaks below the embankment. However, as they were about to launch from the shore, Julie realized her life jacket remained in the tent. Greg said he would retrieve it. He ran back to the campsite, a trip that took about twelve seconds, furiously unzipped the tent door, and crawled inside. By then the smoke was so thick he couldn't see what he was grabbing at. He felt sleeping pads, clothes, and a sleeping bag. After more blind shuffling, his hand landed on Julie's life jacket. He grabbed it and fled, not bothering to zip up the tent. By the time Greg descended the embankment and returned to the shoreline, the fire was in the campsite.

"It was above me," Greg said. "It was like a blowtorch coming across the top of the bank."

Julie was waiting near the shore when Greg returned, the inferno now descending upon them. She had one foot in the shallow water and one foot in her kayak. Greg threw the life jacket to Julie.

"After that, I told her to get the hell out of there," Greg said.

Julie put the life jacket on one shoulder and pushed off as the fire crested the hill behind Greg and flames shot over their heads and out over the lake. Greg quickly lost sight of Julie in the smoke, even though she'd paddled only a short distance from shore. As he was putting his last dry bag in the kayak and getting ready to push off, a sudden gust of wind temporarily lifted the smoke from the surface of the lake. There, in the distance, he could see Julie, about thirty yards from shore. In that moment, the wind literally lifted Julie and her kayak out of the water. Greg estimates the kayak, still carrying his wife, lifted about a foot from the surface. As it crashed back to the water, Julie was ejected. Almost instantly, the kayak stood upright on the stern, barreled end over end, and vanished into the thick smoke. Everything appeared as though it was happening in black and white, like some haunting cartoon from the 1920s.

Having witnessed this terrible imagery, Greg tried to paddle across the lake to reach Julie. She was still at least twenty-five yards away, floating in the water. She had her life jacket on. The wind was too intense to make any progress, so Greg rolled himself from his kayak and into the water. He held on to the watercraft with one hand and pulled through the water with the other. Eventually, he reached Julie. They both held on to the one remaining kayak.

The fire was now surrounding them. Nearby islands, even small ones with just a few trees, were on fire. The shoreline of the lake was a towering inferno. The air was thick with ash and glowing embers. They breathed through a fleece long-sleeved shirt. On occasion the heat and smoke became so intense they had to duck their heads underwater. The water was cold.

As this cycle continued for the next forty-five minutes, Julie started to shake uncontrollably. The longer they were in the water, the more intensely her body trembled. Greg knew she was becoming hypothermic. The shoreline was still on fire, so the best option they could think of was to find some shallow water to stand in. They drifted toward a peninsula that stuck out from the mainland like an extended finger. Eventually they could touch the bottom. They slowly walked through chest-deep water to several nearby boulders and crawled on top of the largest one. Finally they were out of the water. Exhausted, they tried to gather their composure. And then the plume broke.

Wildfires are amazing. They can generate their own weather. Smoke and heat from wildfires create something known as fire clouds. When these clouds mix with cool air in the atmosphere, they form ice crystals. Once the air becomes too heavy, it crashes back to the surface of the earth. On the way down, the ice turns to rain or hail or both. Within thirty seconds of reaching the boulders, Greg and Julie were being pounded by rain. After the sky unleashed a pressure-washer force of dark rain, the rain changed to hail. The couple grabbed a deflated air mattress from Greg's kayak to use as a makeshift roof while they sat huddled on the boulder. There was also thunder, lightning, and more intense wind, all generated from the fire cloud, known scientifically as a pyrocumulonimbus type of cloud.

The pounding rain and hail, though maddening for the paddlers, managed to extinguish the fire. The situation ended as quickly as it began. The skies cleared and order was restored, though the forest was now black where just hours before it had been green.

Their campsite and tent were completely destroyed by the fire. It was getting late, and Julie was still shivering, though not as badly as before. The couple moved from the top of the boulder to the edge of the nearby peninsula. A moment later, one of their dry bags washed up onshore. Inside the bag was a tarp, one sleeping bag, a cooking stove, and some supplemental clothing. They didn't find their food bag, but inside the pack they discovered a piece of leftover cherry pie inside a hard plastic container, the remains of dessert from their first night in camp. Using the tarp, they built a temporary shelter on the peninsula and spent the night there, huddled together in the same sleeping bag.

"It was a little intimidating to still be out there," Greg said. "But we really didn't have a lot of choice at the time."

The next morning, Julie's kayak, the one that had eerily waltzed across the lake, was visible down the shoreline, not far from the peninsula where they spent the night. They retrieved the kayak and immediately started to paddle out of the BWCA. The next lake, Square, was also devastated by the fire. Its shoreline resembled an apocalyptic scene. When Julie and Greg had traveled through the area two days earlier, everything was lush, green, and alive. Now blackened stumps decorated the landscape. It was unusually quiet as they paddled across Square Lake and made their way toward their vehicle, which sat unscathed in the parking area at Kawishiwi Lake. They were alive. Their two daughters waiting back home in Michigan would be able to hear about the experience firsthand from their mom and dad.

First detected on August 18, 2011, the Pagami Creek Fire eventually raged across approximately 93,000 acres of land in and around the BWCA. Though the fire remained alive, smoldering in a bog for weeks, the conflagration grew exponentially following a decision by the US Forest Service to literally add fuel to the blaze. A series of reports, including the extensive document titled "Pagami Creek Fire Entrapments—Facilitated Learning Analysis," shows that the Forest Service severely underestimated the blossoming power of the Pagami Creek Fire during a two-week window in late August and early September 2011. These miscalculations allowed a half-acre burn to grow into a massive firestorm visible from space. Highlighting this underestimation of the fire's power was a decision over Labor Day weekend to dump seventeen hundred gallons of jellied gasoline from helicopters onto the fire. According to the public documents, which date back to the year of the fire, the rationale for the "burn-over" using gasoline includes worsening drought in the region and concern that conditions were too volatile to put crews on the ground. A burn-over is typically done to create a firebreak, or gap, in the hopes of containing spreading wildfires. In this case, the plan did not work properly.

The *Ely Echo* newspaper published an editorial in 2023, nearly twelve years after the fire was put out, that showcases some of the angst still brewing in certain circles near the BWCA. The editorial reads, in part: "First and foremost, this fire could've been a minor footnote. That is before the Forest Service used helicopters to spray over 1,700 gallons of jellied gasoline on the fire up the Fernberg.

"After the *Echo* questioned Forest Service officials, the decision makers had to admit this massive mistake, but since then the fact has been covered up and or forgotten. We can't decide which is worse.

"We'd also point out that decision makers nearly killed six Forest Service employees. There were mistakes made and six people were near[ly] burned alive. At least for this harrowing incident, the full report on what really happened during the Pagami Creek fire finally came to light five years later."

Looking back, Greg and Julie Welch were not the only people who nearly lost their lives during the Pagami Creek Fire. A team of Forest Service employees who were traveling through the BWCA interior to share information about the fire was also in grave danger. A video posted online in late November 2016 details what happened. According to the Forest Service reports and the stories of the six interviewed in what is essentially a short documentary, on September 12 the six wilderness rangers were making public contacts to ensure that no recreationists were in an area of the BWCA that had been closed due to safety concerns. Kawasachong Lake and the Kawishiwi entry point were not included in the closure area.

Anthony Petrilli works on the design and safety of fire shelters for the US Forest Service. He recorded the video of the six wilderness rangers as they explained what happened during the fire. The interviews were conducted in 2012 by Petrilli and Lisa Outka-Perkins on Lake Insula, where the narrow escape involving the US Forest Service rangers had occurred one year earlier.

The wilderness rangers interviewed in the thirty-five-minute video are Nancy Moundalexis, Todd Stefanic, Chris Kinney, Andrea Lund, Nancy Hernesmaa, and Naomi Weckman. They explain in great detail what happened as the fire approached on September 12. The climax of the stories comes as the crew deploys their fire shelters, which resemble large blankets covered in aluminum foil. Four of the rangers had taken refuge on a tiny island on Lake Insula. Two others, Weckman and Hernesmaa, abandoned their canoe and deployed their shelter while in Lake Insula, relying on their life jackets to keep them afloat.

Recalling the incident, the six wilderness rangers describe burning embers shooting through the sky like laser beams, almost no visibility from heavy smoke, and a disturbingly dark sky. Similar to Greg Welch, the rangers liken the sound of the approaching fire to that of an oncoming train. Weckman and Hernesmaa also describe hypothermia setting in while they hid under their fire shelter in the lake. When the fire finally passed and they could emerge from the lake, hail started to pound the women from the sky.

When I spoke to Petrilli in 2016, he did not want to comment on the specifics of Forest Service policy regarding fire management of Pagami Creek or any other fire. He said the video featuring the six wilderness rangers was created specifically for educational purposes to be used by the federal government and other firefighting agencies. The same went for Moundalexis, who insisted her comments were about her lived experience, not policy. Many BWCA visitors will likely recognize Moundalexis from the safety videos the Forest Service requires people to watch before entering the wilderness. The woman with long brown hair who talks about where to bury your fish guts in the Boundary Waters: that's Moundalexis.

And while Forest Service fire-management policies were under question immediately after the Pagami Creek blaze—fanned by its price tag of $23 million—the video was the first public play-by-play of events as told by the six wilderness rangers whose lives were in danger on September 12, the same day Greg and Julie Welch were almost killed. Around the time Greg and Julie were floating in Kawasachong Lake to escape death, the crew of six Forest Service members had to deploy emergency fire shelters as the Pagami Creek blaze approached.

Other than countless "ten years after the fire" reports from the press, media attention has focused largely on the size of the Pagami Lake Fire, what happened to campsites in the BWCA, and regrowth of the forest—rather than on the harrowing escape of the six wilderness rangers. Based in Montana at the Forest Service's Missoula Technology and Development Center, Petrilli did not mince words about why this is the case.

"Fire shelters don't make the news unless they don't work and people die," he said. "But when people live, yeah, it's not going to make the news."

Moundalexis told me not as much about fear as she did proto-col. Safety, she said, was the constant, primary objective as the fire threatened the lives of human beings in the Boundary Waters.

"I just feel extremely relieved that no public or Forest Service employees were seriously injured in the fire," she said.

According to the Minnesota Department of Natural Resources, the Pagami Creek Fire was the seventh-largest fire in state history. It was the biggest fire inside state lines in nearly a hundred years. The powerful blaze vaporized trees and resulted in a towering 35,000-foot plume. Smoke from the Pagami Creek Fire drifted as far as Chicago. All told, the Pagami Creek Fire destroyed numer-ous campsites and rendered many canoe portages and trails unusable and unsafe within the federally protected wilderness. But despite its immense size, the Pagami Creek Fire caused no serious injuries or human deaths. And for the six Forest Service employees interviewed in the video, the memories of what hap-pened on September 12, 2011, remained vivid more than five years later.

"As strange as it may sound, as far as being out on Insula, I still feel awed and humbled by the power and immensity of that fire," Moundalexis said. "And I will never forget what it was like out there that day."

Lee Frelich, director of the University of Minnesota Center for Forest Ecology, told me the Pagami Creek Fire burned approxi-mately 9 percent of the entire BWCA before it finally went out. The fire's severity was the result of extended periods without rain, unusually warm temperatures, and high winds that combined to create explosive fire conditions across much of Minnesota, particularly in Superior National Forest, in 2011. Similar condi-tions in 2021 led to a complete closure of the BWCA, with the Greenwood, John Ek, and Whelp Fires all burning in and around the wilderness that August.

Meanwhile, Greg and Julie continue to paddle in the Boundary Waters. The experience shook them, but it won't keep them from their favorite wilderness destination.

"Anytime you go through something like that," Greg said, "it kind of forces you to reflect a little bit on life in general. It was one of those crazy events that if you make it out, which we did, you really get to know how much you appreciate the things in your life, like your kids and your whole family. It puts everything in perspective, a situation like that."

||

Five years before lightning struck in a shallow bog and led to the slow start of the Pagami Creek Fire, another massive wildfire reshaped the landscape of the Boundary Waters. This one did not start from lightning. It started from a campfire.

On the morning of May 5, 2007, Sue Ahrendt woke up early in her home on the Gunflint Trail and thought about fire.

"Well, it had been hot and dry," she said of the conditions that spring. "And so, Andy and I had been talking actually the day before about 'Oh wow, what if we had a fire right in our neighborhood?'"

In 2007 the Ahrendts were the owners of Tuscarora Lodge and Canoe Outfitters. On the morning of May 5, Sue and Andy were correct in their assumption that where there's smoke, there's fire. That morning, high winds and dry conditions would morph a casual campfire into something amazingly powerful and destructive.

The escaped campfire, which became known as the Ham Lake Fire, would burn for more than a week, torching more than 140 structures in Minnesota and burning 76,000 acres of forest. The fire spread in the BWCA and Superior National Forest along the Gunflint Trail and into Ontario. There was little that could be done to slow the fire as it jumped from lake to lake, relentlessly charging up shorelines and back and forth across the international border. A collection of people along the Gunflint lost their homes. Businesses lost equipment and buildings. Memories were both made and burned away. At the time, it was the largest and costliest wildfire in Minnesota since 1918.

The campfire that eventually became the legendary blaze was started by Stephen Posniak, a resident of the Washington, DC, area. For all of his adult life Posniak had a deep passion for the Boundary Waters. In fact, he lived for his annual canoe trips to the BWCA. Posniak took the canoe-country adventures so seriously that he would essentially train in the "offseason" by carrying heavy objects up and down the alleys near his home in the nation's capital.

In 2007 Posniak was on the third day of his annual spring canoe trip when the fire started. It remains unclear how the fire escaped Posniak's grate at his campsite on Ham Lake—likely just a strong gust of wind—though there is no question he was the person who started the fire.

George Humphrey is a local contractor in Grand Marais who uses heavy equipment for assorted tasks up the Gunflint Trail. At the time of Posniak's trip, Humphrey was under contract to work with and support the US Forest Service during natural disasters such as a wildfire. Not long after the first reports of the fire came in, Humphrey was on the scene at Tuscarora. There, he met Stephen Posniak.

"I was getting [the] dozer inspected by the Forest Service, and this gentleman came up to me and was telling me about the fire and how it started," Humphrey said.

During the brief conversation, Posniak tried blaming someone else for starting the fire. Posniak told Humphrey he was camped near some students from the University of Minnesota who were doing fieldwork and testing the water quality of the nearby lakes. As they spoke, Posniak told Humphrey he tried to put out the fire using "a water bag," part of his portable filtration system.

"He told me he kept going back and forth to the lake filling this thing up, trying to put the fire out," Humphrey said. "But it was more than he could do."

And so the fire grew. By that afternoon, the Ham Lake Fire was blazing its destructive path toward Seagull Lake and the end of the Gunflint Trail. Word traveled throughout the local community and beyond that something dangerous was happening in the Boundary Waters. Mike Prom, co-owner of Voyageur Canoe Outfitters along the Gunflint Trail and Voyageur Brewing in Grand Marais, was the assistant fire chief for the Gunflint Trail Volunteer Fire Department during the Ham Lake Fire. Prom was among the first responders to arrive at Tuscarora. He coordinated with the Cook County Sheriff's Department to get an evacuation order in place. Road closures went into effect.

"We were some of the first ones to get up there, and we knew this was going to be serious," Prom said. "And sure enough, it was."

That night, Sue Prom, Mike's wife and a fellow member of the volunteer fire department during the Ham Lake Fire, needed to get from the end of the Gunflint Trail to Grand Marais. Their children were in town, and after a day of working to protect structures, homes, and businesses, Sue made a drive she'll never forget. Just past the Seagull Guard Station, located about fifty miles up the Gunflint Trail, she seemingly crossed into another world. Fire was burning on both sides of the Gunflint. The road was so hot it was literally starting to melt, Sue said.

"There was some really intense heat. And I thought, *Oh my gosh, my tires are going to melt or my tires are going to pop*," Sue recalled. "I could feel heat coming in from the windshield. I was kind of ducking down below my dash because I didn't know how hot it would get. And I remember praying like, *Please help me get out of this.* Because if anything would have happened, I probably wasn't going to survive."

As she continued to motor down the Gunflint Trail, she eventually reached a checkpoint staffed by more volunteers from the fire department, in addition to law enforcement officers. Dan Bauman was the fire chief on the Gunflint Trail at the time of the Ham Lake Fire. He was standing at the checkpoint and wanted to hear how the conditions were a few miles up the road.

Sue said, "I rolled my window down when I got through there, and he was like, 'Hi, are you okay?' And I'm like, 'Yep.' And he looks and he said, 'I don't think I've ever seen Sue Prom look scared before, but you look scared.' And I'm like, 'Yep. Terrified.'"

Despite the efforts of a variety of agencies and volunteers, by Sunday morning, May 6, the fire was on a path of destruction as it continued north. Sprinkler systems saved some of the cabins along and near the Gunflint Trail. Other structures, including family cabins, burned to the ground. Voyageurs Canoe Outfitters at the end of the Gunflint Trail lost three cabins used for employee housing. In addition, Mike Prom said, the business had "sixteen Kevlar canoes that were a little pile of ash and some aluminum gunnels."

By the middle of the week, May 8 and 9, the fire was roaming the wilds of Canada, mostly on Crown land. It showed little signs of slowing down. In an attempt to cut off its path should the fire return stateside, fire crews intentionally burned a patch of forest on the north side of Gunflint Lake. While this fire was set with noble intentions, the good will of humans is tiny compared with the forces of a raging wildfire. On Thursday morning, May 10, the Ham Lake Fire returned to the Gunflint Trail area. It roared past Gunflint Lake, sending business owners and local residents scrambling for safety. Now back in the United States, it was moving toward the middle of the Gunflint Trail area.

By this time, media coverage of the Ham Lake Fire was extensive, making national headlines and capturing the attention of Minnesotans from the Twin Cities to Duluth and certainly in Grand Marais. WTIP radio provided near-continuous updates of the fire, with host CJ Heithoff staying on the air for extended shifts, including an all-night marathon of live coverage during the fire's peak.

Eventually the Ham Lake Fire would relent. It took rain, cooler temperatures, calmer winds, and the work of, at one point, some one thousand firefighters from the United States and Canada. The ordeal exhausted local, state, and federal resources. The fire's intensity and duration also took a toll on the Gunflint Trail community.

"It was a week of hell from the standpoint that you didn't get a lot of sleep," said Michael Valentini, another volunteer with the Gunflint Trail Fire Department. "Your meals were sporadic. You didn't know what you were doing from one day to the next. And the labor was very, very intense."

On October 20, 2008, Stephen Posniak was charged by the US Attorney's office for crimes related to the Ham Lake Fire. The charges came nearly eighteen months after he accidentally started what would become the massive wildfire.

About two months later, on December 16, Posniak took his own life. He used a gun to kill himself in the backyard of the home he shared with his wife in Washington, DC. Following his death the federal charges—which included leaving a fire unattended, providing false information to a federal officer, and one count of setting timber afire—vanished.

Posniak's attorney, Mark Larsen, called the government's case "an exercise in overcharging," according to the *Washington Post*. In some instances, people who accidentally start a wildfire are not charged with a crime. If arson, or intent, is involved, it can be a different story. Take, for example, a situation in 2017 where an Oregon teenager threw fireworks into a stand of trees near the Columbia River gorge, an act that resulted in a devastating 47,000-acre wildfire. In 2018 a judge determined the fifteen-year-old boy had to pay $36.6 million in restitution. In court the boy's attorney argued that the amount was "cruel and unusual punishment," according to a report from National Public Radio.

In an interview with the *Post* not long after Posniak's death, Larsen said there was no evidence "at all" that Posniak intentionally set the Ham Lake Fire. Larsen said Posniak would have contested the charges "vigorously in court."

Despite many brushes with disaster, there were no official deaths as a result of the Ham Lake Fire. However, many consider Posniak's suicide in 2008 a fatality that resulted from the fire. Valentini, who continues to live at the end of the Gunflint Trail and is involved with the local fire department, is among them.

"There are people who come to the Boundary Waters every year because this is their mecca. This is where they unite with nature. This is their holy grail that they come to," he told me.

Valentini, who has a cabin on Saganaga Lake at the end of the Gunflint, watches year after year as groups, many of them repeat visitors, travel to the Boundary Waters or Quetico. Most of the paddlers who enter Quetico through the Cache Bay Ranger Station go directly past Valentini's cabin, for example. For this long-standing member of the local fire department, the fire stirred empathy.

"This is the place he loved," Valentini said of Posniak. "And then, all of a sudden, something very tragic happened. And I don't know the specifics of how it happened. But a campfire got away from him. And it could happen to absolutely any of us. But the conditions were just wrong that day. And it got out of control. And now the place that you love, the area that you love, you're looking at it, and it's on fire. And my heart goes out to Steve Posniak, who actually was the lone person who died as a result of the fire. And I can't imagine the burden he must have carried after the fire until he tragically ended up committing suicide as a result of it. And, you know, was he responsible for the fire? Technically, yes. But it was an accident. Accidents happen. Bad things happen to really good people. And in this case, that's what happened. And I can just imagine how I would feel in his boots."

If you meet Valentini at Trail Center Restaurant on the Gunflint or at the hardware store in Grand Marais, he's bound to make a wisecrack or two at your expense. Well over six feet tall and with gray, curly locks, he is a valued member of the Gunflint Trail community. He gets involved in fundraisers for the fire department and is often among the first to respond to emergencies, including fires. And he understands that local residents, people who live near the Boundary Waters, are not always the wilderness-savvy saints they sometimes portray themselves to be. And in the long run, losing one's cabin is not the same as losing one's life.

"We've all done things in the Boundary Waters, I would assume, that may have been a little bit questionable. And in this case, the tragedy was the Ham Lake Fire was created," Valentini said. "And I in no way want to minimize the personal loss that people had with property and possessions. That had to be very painful. I know a lot of neighbors who lost everything they had. And it was very painful. But this world is full of calamities and tragedies, from floods to earthquakes, or hurricanes to forest fires. And as a community, and as individuals, we have to recover and respond."

Jane Comings is the widow of Stephen Posniak. It was Comings who found Posniak's body in the backyard of their Washington, DC, home. She spoke with me in 2017, ten years after the fire. By then Posniak had been dead for nine years. In our telephone conversation Comings told me about what Posniak missed out on when he made the choice to take his own life and how his death traced back to his small campfire in the Boundary Waters, the one that got away. Four months after he committed suicide, his daughter, Beth, got married. In subsequent years, Comings said, her late husband "has missed knowing his granddaughter Sylvia and his grandson George."

Comings agrees with Valentini that Posniak was the lone human fatality that resulted from the Ham Lake Fire. Over the years, she said, people who live on the Gunflint Trail have reached out to her and expressed sympathy. For example, an eighty-six-year-old woman whose family cabin burned up in the fire sent Comings a letter that made no mention of blame, but only hope. The woman said her family's cherished bible was lost in the fire, Comings explained, but also noted that things can be replaced. Things can be reborn.

Ultimately, Comings believes Posniak committed suicide "out of shame." He was a very private individual; the criminal charges and the notion that he might have been so careless as to burn down a big section of the Boundary Waters was too much for him to carry.

"What I would need to say about Steve is that he probably treasured his time in the Boundary Waters more than anything else he did all year," Comings said. "It was a wonderful place for him. And there's no way in the world that he would have deliberately made the place less beautiful and less welcoming. But I guess my feeling is that, well, life isn't fair. And sometimes little actions can have disastrous results. There really isn't any rational explanation. Bad things can happen to some people and not to others."

III

Ricky DeFoe intently watches the orange flames dancing near the white snow. Icy waves on Lake Superior roll nearby. These familiar sights and sounds have been witnessed for generations by the Anishinaabe people who live here. DeFoe, an elder from the Fond du Lac Band of Lake Superior Chippewa (also known as Ojibwe, or Anishinaabe), looks to the north as smoke from the small fire made of birch and maple drifts overhead.

"This fire was made in a good way. We made our tobacco offerings. The tobacco that was given from Joe, brought as a gift. There is a lake trout here," DeFoe said. "We want to honor the spirit of the fish."

The lake trout was from Duncan Lake, a popular body of water in the mid–Gunflint Trail area. I had been ice fishing the day before and brought the trout to DeFoe as an offering of gratitude. I'd come to Duluth to talk with DeFoe about fire, both small ones like the one we shared and large ones that have made headlines across Minnesota and beyond during the past two decades, including the Pagami Creek and Ham Lake Fires. More recently, in 2021 the Greenwood Fire burned nearly 27,000 acres and led to a temporary closure of the BWCA.

And while wildfires are viewed by some simply as destructive forces of nature, they played a significant role in shaping what today are considered the most stunning landscapes across the Boundary Waters. The reality is this is a place where wildfire is common—even necessary.

Historically, some of the most important fires the Boundary Waters landscape experienced were those started intentionally by the Indigenous people who have lived here for centuries and who used these fires as a tool of sorts. Other times the fires started naturally, from a lightning strike, for example. Across the 1854 Ceded Territory, a vast area of land in northeastern Minnesota that includes all of Superior National Forest and the BWCA, Indigenous people have for generations engaged in the practice of intentionally lighting smaller, controlled fires with specific outcomes in mind, including acquiring food and clothing, making canoes, and following other means of living with the land known as "cultural burning."

"Fire comes in many forms. Lightning strikes cause some fires. This is natural law," DeFoe says near our winter fire in Duluth. "We say new growth. The forest needs fire to regenerate. It's not always destructive. When we see the ceded territories—the Ojibwe ceded vast amounts of territory to the US government—and we see the mismanagement, the squandering of the wealth of these lands, it's kind of sad. And the traditional and cultural practices of fire use, as a utility in these forests, are needed again. For some reason there's still that piece where they look down upon Indigenous peoples, and the knowledge that we carry, as inferior. And that seems to be a long-held problem here in America."

Regardless of how alarming a wildfire might be, even in a remote setting, a team of researchers from the Upper Midwest is currently asking if select fires should be allowed to burn in order to create healthy forests in certain pockets of Minnesota, particularly in and around the Boundary Waters. Furthermore, the researchers are exploring the notion that perhaps humans should be the ones starting some of these fires in the forest, as was done historically.

Evan Larson, a dendrochronologist and professor at the University of Wisconsin–Platteville, said fire is a "fundamental factor of northern forests." In simpler terms, this means the species that grow in the Boundary Waters and elsewhere, including red pine, jack pine, and other trees and plants, have evolutionarily adapted to fire. As have animals such as moose.

Over the past decade, Larson, along with professor Kurt Kipfmueller and research specialist Lane Johnson from the University of Minnesota, has been leading the research analyzing the historical use of fire in the Boundary Waters. Their explorations focus on what it would mean if landscapes we now consider wilderness were, at least in part, the legacies of human activity.

Though now frequented year-round by visitors from all over the world, the area referred to as the Boundary Waters along the Minnesota and Ontario border is a land long inhabited by Minnesota's first resident and Indigenous communities. This history dates back some ten thousand years to when ancestors of modern Indigenous people hunted and gathered here. Over the course of thousands of years, Native populations moved in and out of the region, including most recently the Ojibwe people. Despite the comings and goings of various human inhabitants, the one constant in the history of the area that is the Boundary Waters is fire.

"We know that Anishinaabe groups in this region have used fire and engaged with the landscape through the process of fire for a host of reasons, whether it's opening travel corridors or maintenance of blueberry patches," Larson said. "And so, we know that there are relationships here."

The team's research area includes more than seventy locations inside the BWCA. Though their work is groundbreaking in how it could impact forest management, the researchers are quick to point out that it builds on that of iconic Minnesota forester and BWCA legend Miron "Bud" Heinselman. A US Forest Service researcher, Heinselman spent a lot of years in the Boundary Waters. He published some of the most important papers in the early field of fire ecology, and he offered up formative ideas for thinking about fire as a process in forest ecosystems. Over the course of his many years of research, Heinselman made a collection of maps illustrating the areas where fires occurred.

Literally following in Heinselman's footsteps, at various stages of the ongoing study Larson and his collaborators traveled by canoe and on foot across the BWCA, using handsaws and other nonmotorized tools to study dead trees as they looked for evidence of fire. It was a laborious task, Larson told me. The hard work was made easier by knowing that their research had the potential to reshape policy, or at least influence it. The data collected shows, among other things, how fire could and perhaps should be used within the popular wilderness area.

The patterns illustrated by the team's data show that fires were most common along the northern border of the Boundary Waters. In some places, the iconic stands of red pine BWCA paddlers see today experienced fires every five to six years during the 1700s and 1800s—the period when fur-trade networks were expanding across the region. While the driving narrative behind the research is the history of fire in the Boundary Waters, Larson says that along the way, the closer they looked at the forest, the more they learned about how this land has been embraced by humans for centuries.

With this understanding, it's worth questioning why people are so afraid of fire in and around the Boundary Waters. Of course, the idea of being burned to death by a raging fire is terrifying. Yet that's not what actually happens most of the time. The stories of Julie and Greg Welch and of the six wilderness rangers during the Pagami Creek Fire are extremely rare exceptions. Nobody died during the Pagami Creek, Ham Lake, or Greenwood Fires—at least not while the fires were burning. Furthermore, essentially nobody was injured during these large wildfires, or any other wildfires in recent memory in the BWCA or Quetico. For many who own property near the edge of the federally designated wilderness, the fear of fire comes from concern over losing their cabin or their home. That's a rational response on one level, but these cabins were built in a forest that needs fire in order to be healthy.

Andy McDonnell from Tuscarora Lodge and Outfitters on the Gunflint Trail said wildfires aren't something that should strike fear into canoe-campers in the Boundary Waters. The thing about wildfires, McDonnell said, is that people typically have a chance to get away from them before they get out of control. A person on a trip to the Boundary Waters is much more likely to drown or be killed by a falling tree than they are to die during a wildfire, McDonnell told me. No stranger to wildfires in the BWCA, McDonnell was among a group later known as the "Seagull Seven" during the Ham Lake Fire. These seven people, including McDonnell and his father, Jack, refused to evacuate from their cabins on Seagull Lake at the end of the Gunflint Trail. As the Ham Lake Fire rolled across the Seagull shoreline, the group worked to save not only their own cabins but those of their neighbors. They turned on sprinkler systems, kept backup generators going so the sprinklers would continue to function when the power went out, and stayed put while the fire moved in. The warlike sounds of propane tanks exploding from heat and pressure, planes landing on the lake to get water, trees falling, and structures burning kept them company during the peak of the fire at Seagull. They all survived. In fact, nobody in the group was injured in any significant way.

There's no guarantee of safety on a trip to the Boundary Waters. Wilderness ranger Nancy Moundalexis doesn't say this outright in the *Leave No Trace* video people are required to watch before the US Forest Service will issue them an overnight permit to the BWCA during the quota season that runs from May 1 to October 31. The video explains more about rules and regulations than anything else, but it also includes some basic information on how to stay as safe as possible during a canoe trip to the Boundary Waters. McDonnell, who is also a member of the Gunflint Trail Search and Rescue team, said the Forest Service does a "pretty good job" of getting people out early when a wildfire is burning in the Boundary Waters.

To keep people away from dangerous situations, the Forest Service can, and does, shut down certain areas of the BWCA when a wildfire is actively burning. In fact, closures of the Boundary Waters, either selected areas or the entire wilderness, are happening with greater frequency. Partial closures happened in 2011, 2021, and 2023. The wilderness was completely shut down to visitor access in 2021 for two weeks due to wildfires. These types of closures will likely be more common in the future, as the earth continues to warm and the forests in and around the Boundary Waters continue to change. Lee Frelich from the University of Minnesota Center for Forest Ecology believes areas of the Boundary Waters will turn from a boreal forest into an oak savanna in the coming decades. Indeed, with each passing autumn more oak leaves decorate some of the portages and hiking trails in the Ely area.

Local, state, and federal agencies that have jurisdiction near the Boundary Waters are constantly navigating the balance of keeping people safe and letting the public have their fun. One example is when a campfire ban goes into effect. Similar to closures of the wilderness, campfire bans are becoming more commonplace in both the BWCA and Quetico. There comes a time each summer, typically around the Fourth of July, when the Forest Service, Department of Natural Resources, and local law enforcement need to consider implementing a ban. Campfires were temporarily banned in the BWCA in 2020, 2021, and 2023, for example. Quetico is even more restrictive with campfires, banning them early and often during any given paddling season, including during each of the years listed above.

Going back to the US Forest Service's founding in the early 1900s, the agency has had a nationwide goal to minimize the size and number of wildland fires. A document published in May 2017 by the Forest Service recounts the agency's history of dealing with wildfire. The document describes the period when Gifford Pinchot became chief of the Division of Forestry in 1898. Pinchot worked tirelessly to inform people about the complexities of wildfire, including the fact that fire can simultaneously be viewed as a threat to and a benefit for forested areas like the Boundary Waters. This balancing act continues, though the Forest Service is quick to suppress fire in the BWCA, regardless of where it is located in the wilderness. The John Ek and Spice Lake Fires south of the Gunflint Trail in 2021 and 2023, respectively, were both fought with aerial water drops and containment efforts by people on the ground. The areas where these fires started were remote, more than ten miles from the nearest building or private property. The Forest Service, in each instance, said the dry conditions and chance for the fires to grow and spread rapidly was the reason they needed to be contained.

Recent spruce budworm infestations in and around the BWCA have left thousands of acres of forest with standing dead trees. These dead trees, mostly balsam and spruce, have created a tinderbox in the wilderness. It is a natural cycle, one repeated for centuries: The budworm moves in. The trees die. Later they burn. Repeat. The BWCA is ready to burn. Humans just won't let it.

Another contributing factor to a potentially explosive wildfire in the Boundary Waters is linked to a single day and natural disaster that occurred two decades before the spruce budworm swooped in. During the early-morning hours of July 4, 1999, a series of thunderstorms formed over portions of North and South Dakota. As the day moved along, the storms grew in strength. Some formed into a bow echo and began moving across Minnesota, bringing damaging winds. The "Boundary Waters Blowdown," as the storm came to be known, lasted for over twenty-two hours and traveled more than thirteen hundred miles at an average speed of almost sixty miles per hour, resulting in widespread devastation in both Canada and the United States. At its peak, which happened to be over the BWCA, howling straight-line winds clocked in at a hundred miles per hour. According to the US Forest Service, an estimated twenty-five million trees were blown down during the storm. These trees now either are rotting in the woods, are dry and ready to catch fire, or have burned. If the trees are still a stranger to flame, they are sources of fuel in a forest that thrives on fire.

Former Grand Marais resident Cindy Carpenter-Straub was camped on Pine Lake on the eastern side of the BWCA during the blowdown storm. Her friend group had a tradition of camping on Pine each Fourth of July. Pine is a spectacular lake on the far eastern side of the BWCA, with deep, clear water and steep ridgelines dominating the south shore. The trip had started beautifully, Carpenter-Straub said, with gorgeous weather and good camaraderie in camp. And then, seemingly out of nowhere, the wind intensified. And it kept getting stronger. Moments later, rain started to pound down on their campsite. The wind only grew louder and became more intense. Scattering, the group fled for shelter. Carpenter-Straub crawled under a tarp strung between large white pines. The tarp whipped violently above her head as she used one hand to hold it down and the other to protect her face from flying branches. In what she describes as "an instant," several of the large pines in and around their campsite snapped near the base of their trunks. The towering trees crashed to the earth. Carpenter-Straub was not hit by the thickest part of a tree, but she was trapped under a weblike mess of branches and pine needles.

"I remember hearing someone scream, and then I was just compacted," she said. "I couldn't move at all. There was another gentleman with me, and I could hear him saying, 'I'm okay, I'm okay!' And then I could barely get enough strength to say, 'I'm not.'"

The trunk of a falling pine came within feet of landing on, and likely killing, Carpenter-Straub that afternoon. By some twist of fate, she suffered only minor injuries. Though shook up, Carpenter-Straub and some of her group actually stayed at the campsite for the rest of the holiday weekend.

"It was the annual Fourth of July trip," she said. "I looked forward to it every year and didn't want to cut it short."

Mike Stewart, a meteorologist from the National Weather Service who was working in the agency's Duluth office, said the storm, known as a derecho, dropped nearly seven inches of rain in areas of the Boundary Waters during the single afternoon. Though such storms are rare, Stewart said people should not be surprised if another violent thunderstorm on the scale of the blowdown returns to the most-visited wilderness area in the nation.

"It's going to happen again," he said.

IV

Most of the people who die in the Boundary Waters are white men or women—mostly men. And most of them die in the spring, summer, or fall. It is extremely rare for someone to die in the winter. Andy McDonnell from the Cook County Search and Rescue team attributes the low death rate during the winter to several factors, starting with pure numbers.

"There's just fewer people here in the winter," he said.

And those who do travel across frozen lakes and snow-covered portages are often well prepared for their expedition. It's one thing to drive with a group of friends or your family from the Twin Cities to Ely or the Gunflint Trail, rent a canoe for the weekend, portage one lake in, and set up camp. This scenario plays out routinely, perhaps thousands of times, over the course of any paddling season. It's a whole other thing to rent the gear required for a successful winter camping trip to the Boundary Waters. Pulk sleds, canvas-wall tents, portable woodstoves, snowshoes, warm clothes, thick sleeping bags, cots—the list of necessary gear goes on. Gearing up for a winter camping trip to the Boundary Waters is time consuming. It can take days to prepare for the trip, and even more time to unpack once the adventure is complete.

There's also the sheer intimidation factor that keeps people away from the Boundary Waters during the winter. It gets cold here. Thirty-below-zero-Fahrenheit temperatures descend on this part of the world nearly every winter. Whiteout blizzards. Deep snow. Relentless wind. Winter keeps most people away from the Boundary Waters, particularly when it comes to overnight and multiday excursions.

Despite the dangerously cold temperatures, hypothermia is more common during the paddling season. Tumbling from a canoe into forty- or fifty-degree water in May or October is among the leading causes of death in the Boundary Waters. Most people don't land in the water during the winter; they stay on top of it. The ice on most Boundary Waters lakes is three feet thick by the time March rolls around. Anyone who does fall in, or partially in, typically gets out quickly and has a change of clothes at the ready. Other parts of Minnesota are more dangerous for outdoor winter recreation than the Boundary Waters. The use of heavy machinery is often the reason why. On January 21, 2023, for example, six pickup trucks driven by ice anglers fell through the ice on Lake Pepin on the Minnesota and Wisconsin border. A sergeant with the Goodhue County Sheriff's Office told reporters that a team worked all day and it took until 8 PM to get the final truck towed from the icy waters. Nobody was hurt during the ordeal, as the vehicles were parked and unoccupied when they broke through the ice.

This situation won't happen in the BWCA because for the most part motors aren't allowed on lakes inside the wilderness. Various corridors, including on Saganaga at the end of the Gunflint Trail, allow some snowmobile access, but even that is regulated to a degree that keeps ice anglers and others who enjoy motorized winter recreation away from the BWCA and Quetico.

That's not to say strange things don't happen here.

Early one winter, for example, a woman from Minnesota froze to death on the edge of the BWCA while she was "awaiting signals from flying saucers."

According to an article published by the United Press International (UPI), in late November 1982, "A woman who shivered through a month-long vigil awaiting signals from flying saucers froze to death in a car at the end of a desolate trail along snowy Loon Lake."

The lake, located almost directly off the Gunflint Trail and less than two miles from the BWCA border, is deep, clear, and full of lake trout. LaVerne Landis and Gerald Flach didn't drive to the Gunflint Trail in 1982 to go ice fishing—and not just because lake trout were still out of season. Flach, who was thirty-eight and a resident of West St. Paul, told the local authorities in Cook County "he had been receiving messages through Ms. Landis from some higher power. The most recent message directed them to go to the end of the Gunflint Trail and await further messages," according to the UPI report.

Just forty-eight years old at the time of the bizarre incident, Landis was a widow and the mother of five grown children.

"Ms. Landis wore open sandals, a sweater, slacks and a coat, and her feet and hands were wrapped in torn strips of blanket when she was found dead," Bruce Kerfoot reported to the press.

The son of Gunflint Trail icon Justine Kerfoot, Bruce Kerfoot was among those who responded to the scene. Search and rescue were notified of the situation when Flach made a desperate crawl from the public parking area on Loon Lake to the Gunflint Trail. Also assisting at the scene was Jack McDonnell, one of the "Seagull Seven" during the Ham Lake Fire and the father of Andy McDonnell from Tuscarora Lodge and Canoe Outfitters.

The *New York Times* picked up the story too, running its own version through the Associated Press. When the rescue squad reached Flach on that cold November night, he was suffering from "chills, dehydration and starvation. He crawled a quarter-mile through snow for help," the *Times* reported.

Dr. Michael DeBevic, who treated Flach at the local hospital in Grand Marais, told the press that the Minnesota couple "apparently ran out of food after a week and did not drink any water the last four days of their ordeal because the lake had frozen. They survived on vitamins," according to the *New York Times*.

"He is very lucky to be alive," DeBevic said of Flach. "He went a quarter mile through knee-deep snow, walking and crawling. He was lucky to have survived that in the condition he was in."

After Flach was discharged from the hospital, family members picked him up and drove him to a psychiatric facility in Fargo, North Dakota, according to the *Times* report.

The local authorities in Cook County did not charge Flach with a crime.

"There's no indication of any wrongdoings," Cook County deputy sheriff Frank Redfield said after the incident. "These people kind of believed in flying saucers."

The remoteness of the Boundary Waters has a tendency to attract people with a penchant for abstract thought. Christine Day, a self-proclaimed healer who says she can communicate with extraterrestrials known as the Pleiadeans, told me in 2019 she had a vision on East Bearskin Lake on the edge of the BWCA. In this vision, Day said, she was informed that she needed to buy a cabin on the shoreline of Lake Superior because an area near Grand Marais would serve as a "gateway to the Galactic community." Day views herself as the "Pleiadean ambassador," she told me, and it was the quiet and spiritual connection she felt near the Gunflint Trail and the Boundary Waters that led to her discovery of the Galactic portal.

Others arrive in the BWCA looking to hide out from the world—and not just for the weekend. On a trip to the Brule Lake area in 2019, the well-traveled canoeist Kevin Kramer and I came across a character who seemed destined to land in the next version of *Rambo*, should Hollywood ever produce such a film. The man was filleting a whole mess of brook trout when we encountered him on the shores of Bench Lake, one portage up from Brule. He was wearing green pants and a cutoff T-shirt. We were greeted with a modest grunt, and then the man got back to work, using a razor-sharp hunting knife, no less. Later we discovered he had three locked coolers at the bottom of the portage. His camp, which was set up on a nearby island on Brule, resembled a military barracks, including a small canvas tent and enough gear to survive for months if need be. We figured that was his plan.

Whether a reclusive type or someone seeking otherworldly connections, people do feel certain energies in the Boundary Waters. Various and scattered locations throughout the wilderness have a history of stirring in people what is most commonly referred to as "a strange feeling." The island campsite where Billy Cameron and his friends from Indiana were camped is one such place. Kramer, a commercial airline pilot, has spent the equivalent of months paddling in Quetico, Woodland Caribou, and Wabakimi Provincial Parks in Ontario, plus countless hours in the BWCA. Only once has he mentioned a haunting or strange vibe at a campsite. The island on Tuscarora stirred something in him.

"It felt as though there was another presence," Kramer said. "To me, it didn't feel scary or threatening. Just different. I sort of embraced the feeling and carried on with my stay there. But I could never could quite shake it until I moved the next day."

Various chat rooms where people talk about Boundary Waters experiences, fishing reports, gear recommendations, and more or less any topic related to the BWCA and Quetico include multiple mentions of the island campsite on Tuscarora. One commenter noted they had "the weirdest feeling that someone or something was there, watching us. I had a group of teenagers along, and we looked around, but found nothing. The feeling persisted, so we left. Back at school that fall, I talked to another BWCA tripper, a woman with almost as much experience as I had. She had stopped at the same site, set up camp, had similar feelings, and broke camp at dusk and found another site. She and I both knew we had never felt that way about any other campsite."

I wanted to see the island campsite where Billy Cameron spent his final night in the Boundary Waters and, therefore, as a living person on this earth. I wanted to experience the energy at the island, to get a sense of what others described feeling. I'd been to Tuscarora once before, on Christmas Day in 2021. The lake was frozen when we arrived, and we didn't make it to the island campsite that day. I wanted to return, this time in a canoe. On a hot and buggy day in mid-July 2023, I did just that.

There are a number of ways to access Tuscarora, but the most direct is by parking at Round Lake, about a mile from the Gunflint Trail. After paddling Round Lake, there is a short portage to Missing Link Lake. From there, it's over a mile-long portage to reach the deep, clear waters of Tuscarora. Matthew Baxley and I arrived at Tuscarora Lodge and Canoe Outfitters on a Sunday morning. Owner Andy McDonnell was sitting behind a large desk as we entered the main outfitting post. We had with us Baxley's Kevlar canoe, a well-traveled Wenonah Spirit II, so we didn't need to rent any gear. We explained to McDonnell the objective of our mission, to visit the supposedly haunted island,

and he said he'd heard the rumors about the island campsite. He'd read the online forums where people described strange energy and feeling as though they were being watched by some unknown entity. And of course McDonnell knew Billy Cameron's story and how he died on Tuscarora in May 2020 after the three-person canoe he was in with his two friends capsized near the island.

But when canoe-campers are scared by seemingly strange sounds in the Boundary Waters, McDonnell said it's usually a beaver.

"People at night will hear things on the water, splashing sounds, and maybe they'll think it's bigfoot throwing a rock or something," McDonnell said. "But most of the time it's just a beaver doing what beavers do."

In other instances, people will hear a tree fall during an otherwise calm afternoon, or at night when there is almost no wind. Again, McDonnell said, look to the beaver.

"That's usually what it is," he said confidently.

What about when whatever gives someone pause is not explainable by such simple logic? A heavy feeling hanging over a campsite? Strange vibes? Mysterious happenings? Feeling like ghostbuster sleuths, Baxley and I bid farewell to McDonnell and the team at Tuscarora Lodge and Canoe Outfitters and headed for the island in the BWCA.

The summer of 2023 was a dreadful season for bloodthirsty mosquitoes and biting black flies across the Boundary Waters. The summer started with a drought, including almost no trace of rain for the first three weeks of June. It was also hot, with temperatures continually creeping toward ninety degrees Fahrenheit for stretches of the paddling season. The sky was often hazy, as smoke drifting south from Canadian wildfires led to a seemingly endless cycle of air-quality alerts across the Boundary Waters from June to August. The day Baxley and I paddled and portaged to Tuscarora Lake had all of these summer highlights. It was hot, smoky, and buggy.

As we paddled, I pondered. The thing about religion, or spirituality, or mysticism—call it what you will—is that it's all about convincing the soul what the mind wants to believe. Most people refer to this as faith. The unexplainable—or things that seem impossible—can be justified through the lens of belief. Belief in "something" also provides support during times of grief, transformation, and even the day-to-day grind. That system works for some people, and not for others.

In a wilderness setting some people who would typically classify themselves as nonreligious, atheistic, or agnostic suddenly feel a spiritual sense of connection to the land and water. The raven that just squawked across the lake, for example, could be someone's deceased relative letting them know everything is okay. Feeling this way is not traditional therianthropy, or shapeshifting, but more a sense of connection to the natural world and one's life, the reasoning goes. Dream interpretation. Tarot card readings. Connecting the dots between the known and unknown. People looking for answers, or at least something to help make sense of this tangled web more commonly referred to as life.

All of these thoughts were swimming through my mind as we made the trek from Missing Link to Tuscarora. Baxley was behind me, carrying the canoe down the long and winding portage. I wanted to keep an open mind about what type of energy enveloped the island. Are there spirits that might try to connect with me? Would I feel this strange energy? Was this place haunted?

After the portage, we took to the water. It's a modest paddle, about a mile, from the portage to the island campsite. The lake was calm as we steered the canoe west toward our destination. When we arrived, there was movement on the island. Several things stirred as we idled a safe distance from the shore. We braced for anything. However, we were not greeted by a sasquatch, a spirit, a ghost, or a beaver. Instead, we met Thang Huynh.

Huynh and a group of merry BWCA canoe-campers were just finishing setting up their tents and hammocks on the island. Huynh, who was born in Vietnam and now lives in St. Louis Park, Minnesota, loves the island campsite on Tuscarora. In fact, it's one of his favorite places on the planet. This was his family's second time camping on the island. They stayed there during the busy COVID summer of 2020, he explained. They traveled back to Tuscarora specifically to camp at this site once again.

Baxley and I sat awkwardly in the canoe while we explained to Huynh the reason we were casually hanging out on the edge of the island. Waves pushed us toward land as we talked about Billy Cameron and shared stories of people sensing that the island could be haunted. Baxley's canoe was continually scraping against the jagged shoreline while we spoke, so after a few moments Huynh invited us into camp.

"Are you hungry?" he asked. "Do you want some food?"

It was a kind and generous offer, though Baxley and I declined.

"We packed some sandwiches," I said.

The island on Tuscarora is a quintessential BWCA campsite. It is isolated. Balsam fir trees are abundant. Some are showing signs of spruce budworm infestation, with the tips of the boughs sporting an orangish-brown color. Numerous majestic white pines still stand on the island as well. Rocky outcroppings make the shoreline uneven and jagged, with gradual breaks and slopes leading down to the lake. The middle of the island has a series of humps, some covered in soil, others bare granite. Canoe-campers who are fortunate enough to nab the site literally have their own island, if only for a few days.

The day Baxley and I visited the island, Huynh walked with us past the heart of the group's campsite and the fire grate. We moved deeper into the woods. Once away from the shoreline, we talked more about the feelings other people said they had on the island, and the fact that Cameron capsized just a few hundred yards from where we stood. Huynh expressed sympathy for Cameron and his friends from Indiana. He also said he did not relate to the notion that the island could be saturated with bad energy.

"We just love the place," Huynh said.

After twenty-five or so minutes, Baxley and I bid farewell to Huynh and his friends and family. However, our time here was not complete. We got back in the canoe and paddled to the back-side of the island, which is roughly five acres in size. Out of sight from the campsite, Baxley and I landed the canoe on a flat out-cropping on the southeastern side of the island. We crawled out and took some time to simply sit. And feel. We also ate our turkey sandwiches and some potato chips. It was a beautiful, sunny afternoon in the Boundary Waters. We decided, both in talking with Huynh and while sitting in silence, that the island felt welcoming. Of course, this was simply our experience in this partic-ular place. We were there for no more than an hour. We were not in a position to decide if the island is haunted. We were not in a position to judge how others felt here or what types of experi-ences they had on this island. Baxley and I agreed on this inter-pretation. And then we left.

For many, the Boundary Waters is simply a spiritual place. Lukas Leaf from the Sportsmen for the Boundary Waters organization, a branch of the Save the Boundary Waters campaign, told me when we were fishing for lake trout that the wilderness is "his church." There didn't have to be a higher power or divine entity involved for him to feel that way; this was just the place he felt more connected spiritually than anywhere else he'd been. There are others who feel this way. They have experiences that run deep, that touch their soul in a profound way. Nashville musician Jerry Vandiver is one of these people.

"I've had some surreal moments in the Boundary Waters," Vandiver said.

One of these experiences took place near an expansive rock outcropping on Fishdance Lake. The rocks Vandiver described are adorned with pictographs, ancient paintings on stone walls. The Indigenous people in what is now the BWCA and Quetico used natural pigments, including charcoal, blood, animal fat, and other materials, to create the pictographs here. They are documented at locations throughout the region, including on Fishdance Lake. Located northwest of where Greg and Julie Welch narrowly escaped the Pagami Creek Fire, Fishdance is part of the Kawishiwi River system in the BWCA. The first time Vandiver visited Fishdance Lake was in 2004. A self-described "pictograph junkie," Vandiver said it was "extremely windy" the day he paddled from his camp on Lake Insula to Fishdance. In a solo canoe, Vandiver was struggling with the wind on Alice Lake and Fishdance, but his desire to see the pictographs spurred him. After he had struggled to make progress up the lake, Vandiver said the wind suddenly died down just as he neared the pictographs. Simultaneously, he felt as though someone was watching him.

"I kept looking back, kind of over my shoulder," Vandiver said. "It felt like someone was behind me."

Vandiver spent more than an hour near the pictographs that afternoon. At one point, a large bald eagle landed in a nearby tree, its massive head turning back and forth as it scanned the lakeshore. Whatever presence Vandiver felt on Fishdance Lake during his time there was "benevolent," he said.

"I never felt threatened or anything like that," Vandiver said.

I spent time in Nashville with Vandiver following my visit to the rolling hills of Kentucky to find out where Jordan Grider lived in the woods of Appalachia. As we talked, Vandiver said he is typically not drawn toward the supernatural, or things that can't be explained with science. After all, he has a degree in biology, he pointed out. That afternoon, when he was paddling on Fishdance Lake, something happened, Vandiver said. He's not able to define it, and perhaps there's no reason to. Sometimes it's okay not to have an explanation for what we encounter on Earth. Nonetheless, Vandiver's experience moved him so much he wrote a song about it, appropriately titled, "The Spirit of Fishdance Lake." Vandiver recorded the song, and occasionally plays it live, with Shy-Anne Hovorka, an Ojibwe musician, songwriter, and educator who lives near Nipigon, Ontario, not far from Lake Superior.

Hovorka told me in July 2023 about her passion for water, the planet's most important resource.

"Water is the blood of Mother Earth," she said. "And because it is the blood that feeds all creation, we need to take care of it."

Hovorka feels a meaningful connection to places like Lake Superior and the countless inland lakes of the Boundary Waters region. Hovorka said that, as an Ojibwe woman, she believes "the spirits of the past, the present, and the future are with and around us at all times."

"They're leading us," she said. "Guiding us."

Faced with skeptics, Hovorka said she tries not to hold any judgment. If someone were to question or doubt that supernatural forces made the wind stop when Vandiver paddled up to the pictographs, or that people felt a strange energy at the island on Tuscarora Lake, or that spirits are watching select locations across the Boundary Waters, from Hovorka's perspective that would be their interpretation to make.

"I would tell them, 'Well, this is what I believe in. You can take it or leave it,'" she said. "But if you don't believe in that spiritual connection, and you still feel very strongly that the energy around here wants you to know something, you should listen."

Hovorka said the history of Lake Superior and the Boundary Waters, so rich, so diverse, so interesting, is worth knowing about. She asks the many thousands of people who claim to love the Boundary Waters, "Have you done your homework about the waters here? Do you know some of the history, and not necessarily like the colonial history of the place, but the entire history? If your guts are telling you to go somewhere else, then it could be that you're in a place of spiritual significance, or it was at some point in time, and that energy is still very strong in that area."

If the law of the land followed a simple pattern of who arrived first, all of the Quetico-Superior region belongs to the Native communities who walked the earth here a millennia ago. History, movement, migration, and treaties have told otherwise. Still, many of the same reasons people celebrate the BWCA and Quetico Provincial Park in modern times were integral to the lifestyle of the Indigenous communities who call this area home.

Anna Deschampe is a member of the Grand Portage Band of Lake Superior Chippewa, located on the edge of the BWCA. What many visitors to the Boundary Waters think of as vacation was just a way of life as she grew up on the Grand Portage reservation.

"We would go fishing in all parts of the year, fall, spring, summer, and winter," she said. "My dad was just a really awesome hunter, and so we would go out, we would spend a lot of time when we were little tagging along with him. And in the winter, he trapped, and he taught us how to do that as well, so it was very much a part of our identity growing up and just a part of our lifestyle."

The animals and plants, and the land on which they grow, were so ingrained in the Deschampe household that Anna never tasted beef until she went to school in Grand Marais.

"I had always grown up eating moose meat," she said. "And so, I think an example like that really speaks to this wasn't something that we would do recreationally or just for fun, but it was a very key element in who we are as people and just how we lived [our] lives."

Anna's father, Norman Deschampe, was the longtime tribal chair for the Grand Portage Band of Lake Superior Chippewa. Norman died in February 2019 after serving as tribal chair for twenty-seven years. Throughout his life and during his decades as tribal chair, Norman was a strong advocate for treaty rights and the history of the Indigenous population in the Boundary Waters region. That history was very important to the family growing up, Anna says. And while her father worked with groups like the US Forest Service toward many common goals, Anna describes the band's relationship with the state and federal governments as complicated, though there are shared values when it comes to protecting the land and waters in the BWCA.

"Treaty rights and wilderness protection laws sometimes collide," she said.

At the time when band members signed the treaty, Deschampe said, "there was no foresight that potentially this huge chunk of land where people lived would . . . be hindered, or be vulnerable to this legislation that could potentially hinder access," That legislation involves laws supported by the likes of Sigurd Olson, including the 1964 Wilderness Act, and the more stringent 1978 Boundary Waters Canoe Area Wilderness Act.

"This is an area where people lived," she said. "We're talking about places where people have family connections to, ancestral connections to, where they learn to harvest their food, harvest their medicines, where people are buried, where they have had ceremonial grounds for generations."

Indeed, treaty rights allow access to the land Indigenous people lived on for generations before white settlement. In Canada an Ojibwe band lived inside the area now within the park boundaries following its formation in the early 1900s. A stark example of how the Indigenous communities were treated while the BWCA and Quetico were being established is the story of Chief Blackstone.

About a hundred years before the COVID-19 pandemic, another worldwide health crisis swept across the globe. The 1918 influenza outbreak, often referred to as the "Spanish Flu," killed more than fifty million people around the planet. It lasted for nearly two years and, like COVID-19, impacted life everywhere. The sickness reached inside Quetico, including to an Ojibwe village located deep in the park's interior. The Sturgeon Lake Band Reserve 24C, as it was called by the Ontario government, was located on Kawnipi Lake's Kawa Bay. The village was based at the mouth of the Wawiag River and had a population of about fifty people.

Canadian author and former Quetico park ranger Jon Nelson wrote about Chief Blackstone in his book, *Quetico: Near to Nature's Heart*. In addition to undertaking extensive research about the park, Nelson knows Quetico intimately, having served as an interior ranger for many years. I spoke with Nelson in 2019 about some of this history.

During the winter months of 1918–19, the pandemic came to Kawa Bay, Nelson said. When the influenza arrived, it spread quickly among the band members, swiftly devastating the village. Chief Blackstone, the leader of the band, knew action was required. In the depths of winter, he and his wife set out on snowshoes to request help. Their journey took them toward Saganaga Lake and what is now the end of the Gunflint Trail before they turned southwest toward Ely. From the tiny town of Winton, Minnesota, located about ten miles from Ely, Blackstone was able to get a message relayed to the Canadian government via a communication radio that the village was in need of help. Then Blackstone and his wife strapped their snowshoes back on and began the journey home.

After traveling across the frozen lakes of the Boundary Waters and snow-covered trails, on the north side of Agnes Lake, about ten miles from the village in Kawa Bay, Blackstone suffered a medical emergency, perhaps a heart attack. He collapsed on the frozen lake and died. His wife was able to get his body to shore, and later he was buried somewhere inside what is now Quetico Provincial Park.

And while the request for assistance was successfully relayed to the Canadian government, it wasn't until the following spring that anyone arrived to help the remaining members of the Kawa Bay community. Mary Jane Logan McCallum, a history professor at the University of Winnipeg, describes the relationship between Canada's federal government and First Nations people during the 1918–20 pandemic as being one of "segregation, isolation, and trauma." Expanding on this notion, Nelson wrote that the flu "may well have been the final event of a band whose population had shrunk to just a few families due to earlier outbreaks of disease." One reason the federal government was likely slow to respond to the request for help at Kawa Bay is that by 1918 it no longer recognized the Sturgeon Lake Band Reserve 24C. Without consultation, the reserve status at Kawa Bay had been stripped in 1915 so that Quetico could be "complete," as it were, or without a First Nations boundary dotting the park's interior. It took nearly eighty years, until June 3, 1991, before the park and federal government issued a formal apology for what happened at Kawa Bay.

The concept of "wilderness" rarely evokes the displacement of people and restricted access, but these realities are part of the history of the BWCA Wilderness and Quetico Provincial Park.

Paula Marie Powell is a Cook County resident who grew up on the Canadian side of Saganaga Lake at the end of the Gunflint Trail. Portions of Saganaga sit within both the BWCA and Quetico boundaries. Powell is a descendant of the Lac La Croix First Nations community in Ontario; her great-grandmother was Aquayweasheik, also known as Mary Ottertail. Aquayweasheik, an Ojibwe woman, grew up on the Lac La Croix Reserve before she met Paula's great-grandfather, Jack Powell. The Powell family planted their roots in the region on Saganagons Lake, another massive body of water located just north of Saganaga and Cache Bay in Quetico.

Powell says her family's deep history in the Boundary Waters region was always intertwined with a sense of connection to the land and water where they lived. Her family has run trap lines, fished, and hunted here for more than a century. Powell says that designating a place like the Boundary Waters as an official "wilderness area" changed not just how people could recreate in the place where she grew up but who could live there as well, regardless of the color of their skin.

"When the BWCA became the BWCA, I remember hearing a lot of people having been kicked out of their cabins and stuff," she said. "Indigenous people and white people, and that it was really unfair to the people who lived there."

Ojibwe communities were not the only people to feel that, in designating the wilderness, the federal government forever changed their way of life. Motor restrictions aside, many area landowners had cabins that stood within the wilderness boundaries. After passage of the 1964 and 1978 wilderness acts, the federal government bought these structures and removed them or burned them to the ground. While the wilderness designation will keep the BWCA pristine, it stirred a sense of bitterness for some, Powell says.

"I think that there's a purpose to it, but there is definitely some resentment, or was," she said. "A lot of times, as you probably know up here, it seems like the rules and regulations are being made by people that maybe don't know what's happening on the ground. And I think there's some of that too, because [a] lot of legislative decisions are made by people in meeting rooms and not the people who are actually affected by them. And I think that that's where some of that resentment came from too."

In analyzing the history of what is now the most-visited wilderness area in the United States, Deschampe points to elements of historical trauma for band members—one can think of what happened at Kawa Bay, for example—but she also speaks with a sense of optimism about moving forward toward common goals such as clean water.

"There's generational trauma with these things and you can look at the Boundary Waters as one example of when this happened, and there are so many examples throughout history," she said. "But to the point of having a wilderness and this huge area of pristine and protected land, I would agree that's a good thing. It's important to have these areas where we can continue to practice our treaty rights because that argument can be made as well: If the water gets polluted and these environmental protections aren't in place, then where are you going to practice your treaty rights anyway, right?"

PART IV

Bringing It All Back Home

I

Lingering ice made for a slow start to the 2022 paddling season across the Boundary Waters. From Grand Marais to Ely, a menacing winter held its grip until the middle of May for most of the canoe-country wilderness. Some lakes were locked in ice for a week later than usual; others went ten days or more beyond their median average. Greenwood Lake, located near the far eastern edge of the BWCA, about twelve miles from the Canadian border, didn't lose its ice until May 20.

None of this—the weather, the ice, the cold—mattered much to Mark Zimmer. A Minnesotan from birth, Zimmer is unique in that he spends about five months each year journeying by foot and canoe across the 1.2 million acres of the BWCA. He travels more than a thousand miles each season, some of it paddling, other times walking. He lives primarily on grain and wild game, mostly fish. He drags Rapala lures behind his solo canoe as he paddles along, often catching lake trout, northern pike, or walleye on the many BWCA lakes he visits each year. But he avoids one of the abundant species, he is quick to point out: Zimmer "never eats smallmouth bass." Bass are what people eat when they can't catch walleye or trout, he explains, a problem he does not face. Zimmer knows where to find fish.

During his travels, Zimmer sleeps in a hammock. He changes campsites often, an approach driven by curiosity more than anything else. He doesn't concern himself too much about things like the weather when he's in the Boundary Waters. For Zimmer, the cold start to the paddling season in 2022 meant less time dealing with bugs buzzing around his camp.

One other unique thing about Zimmer and his travels in the Boundary Waters: he does all of this barefoot.

"I get better traction," Zimmer says of his barefoot adventures.

For Zimmer, staying upright is important. If he is injured in the BWCA, he'll be reliant on search and rescue teams to save him, as he does most of his traveling alone. "I see people slip and I see people fall all the time. And of course I do too, but like maybe one time a year compared to how often I see other people. So really, I [go barefoot] for more security. And it's pretty great. It's nice to have your feet on the ground. And you know, wet shoes all the time? No thanks."

The whole barefoot thing also has family ties for Zimmer. "My grandpa typically went around barefoot almost everywhere he went, so it just never seemed abnormal to me to do that," he said. On occasion, when it's particularly cold or just to give his feet a break, he will put on a pair of tennis shoes that he carries in his pack. He swaps out the shoes, nothing fancy, for new ones every few years.

The "Barefoot Paddler," as he's known in the BWCA paddling community, is a short, bearded fellow who speaks quietly and delivers his words with a charming Minnesota drawl. He was born and raised in central Minnesota, about twenty miles from St. Cloud. He's a bit like a character who just stepped out of a Coen brothers' movie. Or if not a Hollywood film, maybe a program that airs on the National Geographic channel, something along the lines of *The Legend of Mick Dodge,* which featured another spirited outdoorsman who often goes barefoot. Mick Dodge became so famous after his show that he can no longer buy groceries anywhere near Seattle without being recognized. Zimmer does not aspire to be the next Mick Dodge. He doesn't want a camera crew following him around. Zimmer doesn't get caught up in all that. He's completely grounded in the reality of himself. And he found a deeper understanding of this reality by spending so much time alone in the Boundary Waters. "It's just nice out here," he says.

Zimmer spends three seasons living in the Boundary Waters each year. He paddles a graphite ultralight solo canoe he bought online in 2020. He travels more miles in the Boundary Waters in a month than most people, even dedicated paddlers, do in a decade. Accolades mean nothing to him, though. He's not looking for fame. He simply enjoys spending time in the woods and in his canoe. He thinks of his time alone in the Boundary Waters as an entertaining way to stay healthy, both physically and mentally. There's no magic to what he's doing, Zimmer says; it's just natural. In addition to being curious about the wilderness around him, he is extremely disciplined and motivated. In modern times, nobody holds a candle to what he does on an annual basis in the BWCA. By comparison, everyone else is just a weekend warrior.

"I've just really grown to love it," he said of his solo paddling and time alone in the Boundary Waters. "I find more happiness here."

Zimmer acknowledged that moments of isolation can become very real in the sense of being alone in a massive wilderness. "It can get lonely because I'm by myself," he said. "I guess the experiences and doing it myself and relying on myself for everything is kind of empowering. So I do it for a lot of different reasons. But mainly because it's a great way to live."

I first met the Barefoot Paddler in 2018 when he was thirty-seven years old. He appeared as a guest on the WTIP *Boundary Waters Podcast*, which I'd cofounded just a few months before for the community radio station based in Grand Marais. Zimmer stopped by the station when he was in town resupplying and recorded an interview with my cohost Matthew Baxley. The three of us spent time chatting before and after the recording. During the interview, Zimmer came across as somewhat sheepish and, perhaps more likely, uncomfortable. After all, there he was, out of his element, in a small recording studio. Four pale walls surrounded him. Artificial light beat down from a fixed structure locked tight to the ceiling. Microphones and cables and wires were strewn about in all directions. To a person who spends so much time in the natural world, the whole scene was uninviting. It was chaos. "I don't necessarily have a goal" was among his most noteworthy quotes during the interview. Profound in one sense, perhaps. But the reality of the interview and our conversations with Zimmer at WTIP is that the experience was like attempting to make small talk with a nervous date in a fancy restaurant. He just wasn't open to talking. He didn't feel comfortable.

Four years later I met up with Zimmer again. This time, it was on his turf: Brule Lake in the BWCA. Immediately noticeable: the energy was different. Zimmer actually looked somewhat different, as peculiar as that seems. And not in the sense that he lost weight or had a darker tan. He actually looked like a different person. His green eyes were alive. Brown locks of hair stuck out from under his floppy, full-brimmed green hat. He wore a brown shirt and blue shorts. More than just a rudimentary beard, his facial hair was a mane covering his cheeks and jaw. And then there were his feet, which were nothing short of spectacular. Covered in a thin layer of dirt even after standing in the water for a few moments, Zimmer's feet are easy to fixate on. They look the way a person's hands look after they've been gardening all afternoon in the sun. There's mud caked to the edges of the nails. A red hue makes the skin on his feet seem glossy, even when they're dry. Zimmer keeps his toenails longer than most paddlers would prefer, a benefit of not wearing shoes. His toes are comfortable because "there's nothing pressing down on them," he explained.

Although in the studio Zimmer claimed not to have any particular goal, the day I met him on Brule Lake he seemed to have clear purpose as he stepped barefoot from his solo canoe and into the shallows near the shoreline. It was a beautiful summer day in the BWCA. White clouds decorated a deep-blue sky. A slight chop on the lake's surface made the sun sparkle in the crest of small waves. I let the natural beauty soak in as Zimmer looked curiously in my direction. Breaking the tranquility of the moment, he spoke: "The bugs aren't so bad," he declared.

For more than a decade, each winter the man known as the Barefoot Paddler works odd jobs, mostly construction, saving his money so he can spend May through September living in the wilderness. When he's in the Boundary Waters, he is at home. When he's away from the wilderness, he feels like just another sucker on the vine. "I understand, to an extent, why things are the way they are in society," he said. "The whole thing with everybody working to make money and all of that, I get it. I just come at things a little bit differently."

Money to obtain food is essentially the only reason Zimmer doesn't live, more or less, in the Boundary Waters. At the start of each season he buys wild rice, which he pairs with fresh fish and various edible plants and fungi. As his season in the wilderness wears on, either he leaves to get more grain or people bring it to him during a resupply. Zimmer's learning to forage mushrooms, a task he takes seriously so that he doesn't eat the wrong kind and accidently poison himself. There's speculation that Chris McCandless died this way in the bus in Alaska, a fate Zimmer is well aware of. "I don't want to go out like that," he says. "I'm okay dying, but not that way."

Each night near his chosen campsite, Zimmer hangs his food bag from a tree. He ties a baseball bat–sized stick to a piece of rope, tosses the stick over a branch from a nearby tree, and then replaces the stick with the bag. He lifts the bag off the ground at least fifteen feet and secures the other end of the rope to the trunk of the tree. He hangs the food to protect it from bears but also from critters like red squirrels and small rodents that might attempt to steal his rations.

For hunting and, to a lesser extent, for protection, Zimmer carries a gun when he is in the BWCA. He used to carry an old Wild West–looking pistol. These days, he carries a Ruger 10/22, a small rifle. It's a backpacking model, one where the barrel comes off and folds back into itself. He's pleased with this upgrade, Zimmer said, "because with the pistol it was really hard to shoot grouse. And now that I have the rifle, I can pick them off a little easier in the fall." But, Zimmer said, it's not necessary for a person to carry a gun to feel safe in the Boundary Waters. Most people think they need a gun to protect themselves from animals. This is simply not true, according to Zimmer, who added that he is not frightened "at all" of wolves, for example. Canoeists in the Boundary Waters occasionally will see wolves. By comparison, someone is much more likely to see a bear or a moose on a canoe trip, and most people consider these encounters to be

magical. Wild animals in the BWCA, most notably wolves, usually run away when they see a person, Zimmer says. An aggres-
sive bear trying to take food is an exception, but shooting the
bear is something Zimmer would do only if he was being
mauled. In 2015 Zimmer backed down a bear that had gotten
hold of his food bag and tried to carry it away. The confrontation
was intense, he admits, but ultimately the bear walked away
without the food. "I won," he said.

In terms of inflating the grandeur of danger, Zimmer said
the fear of wild animals tops the list. Wolves and bears typically
want nothing to do with you. A bear wants your food bag, he
said, but it doesn't want to take a bite of your leg just to satisfy its
hunger. Zimmer has spent more time in the BWCA during the
past decade than even the most dedicated wilderness ranger or
wildlife researcher. He has pretty much seen it all. Bears, moose,
wolves, snakes, spiders, all of the critters that tend to generate a
response from the human nervous system, they all just want to
be left alone, according to the Barefoot Paddler.

Zimmer says other human beings are actually the most fright-
ening thing in the woods. His trepidation has nothing to do with
the wilderness being too crowded or not being able to secure a
campsite. He's afraid of people because some of them don't treat
others with kindness, even in the wilderness. As a case in point,
take the actions of Barney Lakner, an Ely resident with a storied
history of breaking the law in the Boundary Waters, with viola-
tions that include driving a snowmobile across the nonmotorized
BWCA and fleeing law enforcement officials in the wilderness.
At the top of Lakner's rap sheet, however, is a 2007 incident
known across canoe country as "the night of terror."

According to the charges, Lakner, who was thirty-seven at the
time, and five other males, most of them teenagers, were firing
guns and drinking on Basswood Lake near a family's campsite.

According to a 2008 report in the *Star Tribune*, the family, who were vacationing from the Chicago area, had to flee from their campsite and hide in the woods. And, "as they held onto one another, they were forced to listen to the yelling men describe, in extremely graphic terms, how they were going kill [the father of the campers] and rape his entire family." The *Tribune* reports that "the case drew widespread attention because of evidence that it was fueled by lingering resentment among some residents of the Ely area, including Lakner, of the environmental activism that led to creation of the BWCA in the late 1970s."

Additional reports, including a September 17, 2007, article in the *St. Paul Pioneer Press*, explains more about the night of terror: "One family of nine, seven of them children, described how the men swore at them, how one of the men swam naked nearby and how the men refused to leave when [the mother of the children] asked them to." The article continues: "She told the boaters that they had children and asked them again to please leave, a [criminal] complaint said. The boaters only hurled the f-word again. Another family said they heard the men and what sounded like a machine gun and saw a flash of fire. After leaving their area, the boat returned, with the men screaming and laughing. . . . One member of the family heard, 'Here we come,' 'Here comes the cavalry,' and 'You can't hide.'"

During his many nights in the wilderness, Zimmer has never experienced anything even remotely close to the night of terror. The people he meets each year on portage trails and while paddling on the smaller lakes in the BWCA are typically very friendly, he said. As a gesture of kindness, and perhaps as a conversational icebreaker, Zimmer occasionally asks if they'd like a group photo. "Most people out here don't get that group shot with everybody in it," he said. "Somebody is always left out. So it's a good way for me to meet people sometimes, by offering to take a couple pictures."

Zimmer does not carry a water filter when he is in the BWCA. He also does not boil water as a precautionary measure before he drinks it. When he's thirsty, he simply dips his cup or water bottle into the lake and gulps the liquid down. When I asked him why he does not treat his water, his joking response was simple: "Why kill the protein?" Indeed, certain lakes in the Boundary Waters watershed are among the cleanest in the nation. Still, giardia from beavers is a constant threat in nearly every lake. Zimmer is careful not to collect drinking water near a beaver lodge or from a small creek. So far he's been lucky: the water has not harmed him. Well, except for the time he capsized while running a stretch of rapids on the western side of the BWCA. The event left him bloodied and bashed, with a mild sprain to his knee ligaments. Much to the dismay of agencies like the Minnesota Department of Natural Resources, Zimmer rarely wears a life jacket, though he is legally required to have one in his possession while canoeing. Everyone who visits the BWCA on a paddle trip must carry a personal flotation device, and the recommendation is to wear it. Zimmer wouldn't give a specific reason as to his choice not to wear a life jacket when paddling across the BWCA, even when I pressed him on the issue.

"If I do, it's because the water is freezing," he said. "But other than that, it just occasionally gets used as something to sit on. But maybe someday it will help."

In this designated wilderness on federal land, the longest one can camp at a specific site in the BWCA is fourteen days. That's not an issue for Zimmer. He prefers to move constantly, choosing a new campsite nearly daily. And so he's out there, living. And moving. "I've got some different lakes I like more than others, but they're all worth seeing," he said. Zimmer should know: he's visited most of the approximately eleven hundred lakes in the BWCA. "I've been to probably 98 percent of the lakes with a maintained [portage]," Zimmer said. "And I'd say between 60 or 70 percent of the others."

There have been some injuries along the way, mostly minor cuts and bruises. No broken bones. Nothing that cut his paddling season short. Zimmer did contract Lyme disease in 2022; he viewed the illness as more a setback to his adventure than a serious threat to his health. But the situation did cramp his style. Deep in the wilderness at the time, Zimmer had to portage and paddle for miles and then drive to Grand Marais to visit a health care clinic. At Sawtooth Mountain Clinic he was given oral antibiotics and directions from the medical provider that included getting plenty of rest. Zimmer went back to the BWCA within twenty-four hours. "It hurt getting the canoe on my shoulders," he said of being sick with Lyme disease. "Once I got it situated, it was mostly okay."

Zimmer is greeted by thousands of insects each year across the Boundary Waters, though 2022 was the first time one of them forced him to leave the wilderness, albeit for less than a day. The worst part, Zimmer said, was that he had to obtain another permit just to get back into the BWCA. "Damn ticks were pretty bad this year," he said in August 2022.

Most canoe-country paddlers would never consider starting a trip in the spring or summer without some form of insect repellant, but Zimmer is different. "I guess the bugs don't bother me enough to want to use it," he said. And so he deals with swarming mosquitoes, biting black flies, and buzzing deerflies and horseflies for most of the time he is in the woods. The bugs are rampant by varying degrees and fluctuate in their intensity as they hatch. In May and June, it's black flies. In later June and July, mosquitoes. Ankle-biting flies come later. It's all part of the process, Zimmer says.

Spending about half the year in the Boundary Waters means Zimmer is occasionally in some sort of precarious, even dangerous situation. Notable experiences include essentially fighting off the bear that attempted to steal his food bag, avoiding falling trees that crash around his campsite during violent thunderstorms, and paddling across big water rolling with whitecap waves. In other words, the things that could happen to almost any visitor to the BWCA on any given trip. Sometimes, particularly when trees are falling or when whitecaps are rolling, people die. Zimmer, who chooses to live with the dangers that are wilderness realities, has remained alive. At least so far.

"There's some luck involved," Zimmer said. "Something could happen to me any day out here that could reshape everything, or even kill me. I know that. And so, it's luck, and there's planning, being careful about where you step, where you camp, when you paddle, all of that stuff."

Zimmer said he would like to experience the BWCA in winter, when things reset across the region, when the snow flies and the lakes are locked in ice. But he would never consider spending the entire season in the Boundary Waters. "I'm not crazy," he said.

11

The day I met Zimmer on Brule Lake, Matthew Baxley joined the adventure. I brought three twelve-ounce ribeye steaks from Johnson's grocery store in Grand Marais. We made a small fire and cooked the steaks to medium rare. Blood seeped from the meat as we ate. There were no utensils involved: we ate the steaks with our hands, tearing and chewing until there was nothing left. The red meat "was goddam delicious," Zimmer said, a welcome change from the fish he constantly eats when he's in the BWCA.

We kept conversation to a minimum while we ate, primarily so Zimmer could enjoy the iron-rich protein in relative peace. The conversational hiatus also allowed me a chance to soak in the beauty that is mighty Brule Lake. Brule is an impressive body of water. At just over four thousand acres, it's the second-biggest lake located entirely inside the BWCA, behind only Trout Lake near Ely. Saganaga Lake, at the end of the Gunflint Trail, is the biggest lake in the BWCA, but a section of the massive lake is outside the wilderness line, with another portion located in Canada. Brule is home to thirty campsites, some of which can only be described as spectacular. Large pines surround the lakeshore and the many islands of Brule. Clear water and excellent walleye fishing enhance the experience for many anglers. Brule is easy to access during the open-water season, as a large parking lot sits in the southeast corner of the lake. Because of its accessibility, including the fact that you can unload a canoe from your vehicle and simply paddle away without completing even a single portage, Brule could be viewed as a beginner's lake. However, much like Sag, Seagull, Pine, and other lakes that are easily accessible on the eastern side of the wilderness, Brule is full of potential hazards. Among the prominent dangers are wind and waves. This reality literally blew in my face as Zimmer finished chewing the final bites of gristle and charred pieces of fatty steak.

A west wind had been increasing with a fair degree of intensity during the forty-five minutes we sat on the peninsula, conditions Zimmer is mindful of entirely, though he processes his observations without words. After a decade more or less of living here, he's in tune with what's happening all around him in these woods and waters. The only thing unfamiliar with the setting was, well, Baxley and me. "I don't mind having company out here," Zimmer said when I asked him about the experience of sharing this meal together. "You guys are pretty funny." While Baxley interviewed Zimmer for the podcast, I stripped naked and swam up to them on the other side of the peninsula. "Kiss my bare arse, Barefoot Paddler," I said.

Zimmer carries an emergency beacon when he's traveling across the Boundary Waters. He's also got a phone, and he picks up more cell service these days as towers are continually built closer to the edge of the wilderness. "When I first started doing this, I didn't carry a beacon or a phone. Back then, I had to become more comfortable with the fact that if something happened

to me, that I'd probably die, you know? But then I got one of
those beacons. And that kind of changed my attitude toward what
would happen to me out here if I got in a bad situation."

Zimmer keeps a tight list of what risks are real for canoe-
country travelers and which tend to be spun more from imagina-
tion or fear. Cold-water drownings and mistakes running rapids
during high water, he said, are the most likely ways someone is
going to die in the Boundary Waters, particularly early or late in
the season. Trees blowing over and landing on your tent or hammock are also a factor that can lead to serious injury or death,
Zimmer said, rattling down the list as though he's jotted down
these sentences a hundred times. Lightning strikes happen and
can kill someone. Nature does its thing, Zimmer said, and sometimes that hurts.

"Not much you can do in certain situations," Zimmer said.
"Plan ahead and hope for the best."

Then there's broken bones and twisted ankles sustained on the
portages or while getting in and out of the canoe. I told Zimmer
about a friend of mine from Iowa who comes to visit nearly every
summer to go fishing in the BWCA. This friend, he's always catching the toe end of his shoe on the gunnels when he's getting out
of the canoe. Every time this happens, he trips and nearly falls.
It drives me mad, I told the Barefoot Paddler.

"Lift your feet," Zimmer said. "Don't be lackadaisical about
where you put them."

In terms of dealing with the weather and a place known for
its long winters, most people who visit the BWCA are overcau-
tious about the cold, Zimmer explained, catching me somewhat
off guard. Keep moving, change your clothes if you have to,
maybe get to camp and start a fire, you'll warm up, he said, oddly
cheerful.

One thing Zimmer stays away from these days is alcohol. He's had some trouble with drinking, including legal consequences. It has no place on his canoe trips. Alcohol makes you sloppy; it takes you out of the moment, he said. According to the National Institute on Alcohol Abuse and Alcoholism, alcohol impairs judgment and increases risk-taking, a dangerous combination during an extended camping trip. Alcohol, like bug spray, is not something Zimmer carries in his portage pack. "As a soloist, I have to be on top of my game all the time," he said. "And when I first started coming up, ten or twelve years ago, I didn't bring any booze then either. And back then, I was drinking a lot. So it was a way to get away from that. And I guess when you don't even have an option to do things, it's a great way to force your-self to stop. It's not an easy way to do something. But it's an effective way."

Zimmer's mother, Cathy Studer, who lives in Cold Spring, Minnesota, comes to visit her son once per season in the Bound-ary Waters, typically spending a few nights canoe camping and catching up on how the time in the woods is going for Zimmer. Studer told me she is okay with her son choosing to live his life this way, essentially as a seasonal resident of the Boundary Waters.

"I don't worry too much about it," she said. "I know he is car-rying supplies with him and that he would be able to survive even if something happened. And if not, he has, I think, made peace with the fact that if something does happen, and it's trau-matic, then that's what happens."

Zimmer said his mother is much more supportive of his time in the woods than his father, but that his dad "is coming around" on the extended stints in the BWCA. "My dad wants a paved road in life," Zimmer said. "I like a gravel road, one with a few bumps in it. It still leads somewhere."

Studer does occasionally wonder how long she would wait without hearing from her son before she contacted the authorities. While we talked about such a situation unfolding, Studer said she would respond in the moment. In other words, she doesn't waste time thinking of the worst-case scenarios for what could happen to her son when he is alone in the woods. "I don't sit and worry. I don't. I have come to peace with that. The thing is, he's very well prepared. And he's very knowledgeable. And sure, an accident could happen, but I'm just counting on his experience and his preparedness. So it should be fine. And when I tell some people that, they are okay with it. And other people are like, 'Oh my god! He's out there barefoot and by himself for six months!'"

Our steaks finished, the podcast recording complete, and my clothes back on, the wind speed continued to intensify on Brule Lake. We put out the fire and Baxley and I prepared to depart. I asked Zimmer if whitecaps or otherwise dangerous paddling conditions give him pause.

"Are you afraid of drowning?" I asked.

"Not really," he replied.

The podcast episode featuring Zimmer on Brule Lake became one of the most listened to among the now more than one hundred in the production's history. Baxley and I stopped producing the WTIP *Boundary Waters Podcast* in late 2023, though we both continue to share stories from the BWCA for Paddle and Portage, a new company we formed in 2024. During events such as the Canoecopia paddling expo in Madison, Wisconsin, Baxley and I frequently heard from listeners of our podcast who are fascinated by Zimmer's lifestyle choices. Some of the comments carried a touch of jealousy, others genuine curiosity. Nearly all of them had the tone of, *Does that guy really live out there all summer?* Indeed.

Before we parted ways on Brule, Zimmer asked me about some of the stories I've heard or reported on where people died in the Boundary Waters. I told him about Billy Cameron falling from the canoe into the frigid waters of Tuscarora Lake. I mentioned Ben Merry and his family members getting struck by lightning. I described Lloyd Skelton's disappearance from the Angleworm Trail. And then Jordan Grider came up.

"That's the young guy from over by Ely and the wolves and all that?" Zimmer asked.

Zimmer knows the story. Grider was not attacked in the night by a pack of bloodthirsty wolves. He was injured beforehand, bled out, and then he was eaten. I told Zimmer that Grider's brother, Joey, a police officer in Albuquerque, told me they found a big jug of vodka at Jordan's camp near the Sioux Hustler Trail. I also describe the quarters Grider planned to sleep in for the entire winter: a cheap hammock and a thin sleeping bag with a liner. Zimmer shook his head, though seemingly not from disgust. Rather, I could almost see Zimmer envisioning what it must have looked like when the wolves had their way with Grider's body.

I asked Zimmer if thinks about the fact that he could die in the Boundary Waters. The mathematics behind it—time plus chance equals . . . —could lead to such an outcome.

Zimmer paused for a moment and looked toward an anthill not far from his bare feet. A waxing crescent moon hung over a granite outcropping on Brule as the day began to fade. Green conifers lined the shoreline to the south. Several seconds passed before he responded.

"I mean, there's always the possibility," he replied. "Especially when you're alone, which I am all the time, the risk goes up, but, I mean, you have to enjoy life. There's always a risk in just about everything people do."

III

The airport in Albuquerque is an easy place to find your way. Serving a city of more than half a million people, New Mexico's largest airport is a welcome hub after my time spent visiting the Grider family in December 2021. I had spoken at length with Jordan Grider's parents about what the BWCA looks like, what kinds of fish we catch there, and what creatures roam the canoe-country wilderness. Now at the airport, and much to my surprise, the bright lights, the local artwork, the voices of people from all over the world—these sensory inputs are what I need after spending a full day in the house where Grider grew up. After making it through security, I find a spot to order a burrito. The woman behind the counter at Tia Juanita's is friendly as I place my order. "Green or red?" she asks, referring to the type of chile sauce that accompanies many food items in the Southwest. "Christmas," I respond, attempting to appear well versed in the local dialect. She nods, acknowledging my request for both.

I have more than an hour before the boarding process begins for my short flight to Salt Lake City. From there I'll change planes and fly back to Minneapolis. A five-hour drive through northern Minnesota and along Lake Superior concludes the trip, bringing me to Grand Marais and the edge of the Boundary Waters. It's snowed fourteen inches during the five days I've been gone. The labor of snowblowing and shoveling my hundred-yard driveway is waiting for me when I get home. It will be dark outside when I return.

The Albuquerque airport is officially called the Albuquerque International Sunport, a clever brand applied by someone in the tourism industry to showcase the nearly three hundred sunny days the area has on an annual basis. All manner of southwestern decor adds flare. Orange and black on canvas. Earthy tones on cylinder shapes that run to the ceiling. Black prints emblazoned with buffalo on the walls. An original 1914 biplane that took flight in New Mexico hangs overhead in one corner. It's about people, all of this stuff. Culture. After finishing my lunch, I walk around the terminal. A work by New Mexico artist Holly Roberts titled *Coyote with Woman Inside* catches my attention. The oil painting shows a woman emerging from a doglike figure. Two yellow lines create the horizon, with seven scrubby desert trees in the background. The black head of the figure looms in the center of the painting. I think about wolves and being in the Boundary Waters. I remember seeing a black wolf running across Duncan Lake near the Gunflint Trail, snow kicking up behind the animal after it saw me standing on the frozen lake. I think, too, of a black wolf that a Department of Natural Resources conservation officer told me he saw standing on the shore of Star Lake near the edge of the BWCA, and how it stared at him for an uncomfortably long minute while he sat fishing in his solo canoe. I silently stand and look at the painting for about fifteen seconds, then move on.

I settle in a remote corner of the airport and pull out my laptop, send a few emails, and land on YouTube. I open a video I've been meaning to watch titled "Canoeing Accident on Boundary Waters Wilderness River." The video is dreadful. It features six men in three canoes who attempt to run a stretch of rapids on the Little Pony River near the Echo Trail, about forty miles from Ely. One canoe capsizes not long after the party departs Bootleg Lake. Most of their gear enters the water, as do the two paddlers. The current pins their Kevlar canoe against a large boulder, eventually bending and destroying the watercraft. Throughout the nearly nine-minute video, the group makes desperate and dangerous attempts to rescue their wet packs from the rapids.

A young man named Steve Hansen filmed the video, which was posted in 2012. It opens with the warning that "The following was all shot on location. Real people were in danger." Indeed. In one scene, one of the canoers, Pat Elliott, is standing on a fallen white pine in the river. He balance-beam walks the pine intending to retrieve a green portage pack. The pack is soaked with cold water and wet gear, but Elliott is able to drag it from the river. In the next scene, Tom Diedrich is standing in the fast-moving current of the Little Pony River, his Kevlar canoe pinned to the rocks behind him. Diedrich attempts to hurl a backpack toward shore, only to watch it bounce off a rock and then float down the river. Diedrich is nearly swept away himself when he attempts to grab the pack as it floats by. As the footage rolls, the Kevlar canoe finally folds around the rock.

The video is so surreal it almost seems fake. Despite the intensity of the situation, the narrator's tone throughout is monotone, even childish. Hansen watches as friends and members of his extended family face serious injury, seemingly oblivious to the danger looming over every choice being made. Somehow the group makes it out of the situation largely unscathed, though their Kevlar canoe is destroyed. The party of six piles into the remaining two aluminum canoes and escapes the wilderness. More than 41,000 people have watched this video. There's not much one can really learn from it, other than to use portages when they are available, unless you are a skilled paddler comfortable running rapids.

Watching the video puts me in a strange mood. I close the lid of my laptop and slide it into the black and orange backpack I use to carry my work equipment. I'm surrounded by people in the Albuquerque airport who probably know very little about the Boundary Waters. I'm fourteen hundred miles from my home in Minnesota.

What I could not have guessed was that in just over a year I would almost die in the Boundary Waters.

IV

Like the previous year, the ice came out late in 2023. Across the Boundary Waters, anxious paddlers wondered if the permits they had purchased months before were worth holding onto as ice clung to many lakes until the middle of May. Each year in mid-January the US Forest Service makes permits for the upcoming quota season available for purchase. Though overnight permits aren't required until May 1, many visitors to the BWCA essentially book their trips in the depths of winter and spend months planning their adventures. In 2023 I booked an early permit for East Bearskin Lake, on the far eastern side of the wilderness. As the date drew closer, and after carefully assessing the situation in early May, three friends and I decided to book a permit for the Baker Lake entry, located east of the Sawbill Trail, instead. The entry point is essentially a paddle through the upper reaches of the Temperance River. The parking area and put-in spot are located inland about twenty miles before the river crosses Highway 61 and flows into Lake Superior. From its headwaters at Brule Lake, the Temperance drops more than twelve hundred feet as it snakes its way down and eventually into the great lake. While winding through the BWCA, the river occasionally widens into a series of lakes, including the entry point at Baker. Moving up-stream from there, canoeists paddle through Peterson, Kelly, Jack, Weird, South Temperance, and eventually Brule. The river narrows between each lake, creating current. In spring and other times when there is high water, the current is swift through these narrow stretches. Alder, cedar, spruce, birch, poplar, and the occasional pine grow tight to the bank along the narrows. To get around these stretches, there are portages. They begin at the bottom of the flow and end somewhere near the top.

The morning of Friday, May 12, was an exceptionally beautiful day across the Boundary Waters. Temperatures hovered in the low seventies. There was almost no wind. The sun was warm, and whatever clouds happened to float across the sky were white, small, and innocent. The fishing opener in Minnesota was the next day, and our group—Erik Dickes, Kevin Kramer, Matthew Baxley, and myself—was thrilled to be getting back on the water following another long winter. Dickes traveled from Omaha, Nebraska, for the adventure, his first fishing opener in Minnesota. Kramer and Baxley are seasoned BWCA paddlers. Dickes and I hit the water first in my green Royalex canoe. Baxley and Kramer were close behind in another.

Baker Lake is a tiny body of water, more a pond than a lake. The Temperance quickly picks up pace and flows by a small public campground near the launch site. About two minutes after we put in, Dickes and I were climbing back out of the canoe to walk our first portage around the Temperance on our way to Peterson Lake. The river, swollen from snowmelt, was moving tremendously fast. Swift white water rapids churned like a dark, living force. With massive volume, the cold water rolled over large boulders and fallen trees. The ice had come out on these lakes just days before. From all reports, Brule Lake, farther up the river chain, still had ice on it. Our destination on day one was Kelly or Weird, as we assumed each lake would be ice-free. Both had quick access to moving water not far from a campsite, and we knew the walleye were likely to be spawning in the current when the fishing season opened the next day.

The first portage of the trip, from Baker to Peterson, is an easy thirty-four-rod stroll, just over a tenth of a mile through the woods. The pathway cuts away from the river slightly, but it's always within earshot, even when the water is low. That day, with the water extremely high, the roar of the Temperance meant we had to talk somewhat loudly in order to hear each other clearly when we were standing near the river. Dickes and I were the first to walk up the portage. A recently fallen spruce was blocking the trail not far from the takeout on Baker. The tree had the diameter of the thick end of a softball bat. Though we were anxious to get to camp, Dickes dropped his pack and pulled out his cutting weaponry, a twenty-one-inch Agawa folding bow saw with a black frame and green handle.

"Let's clean this up," he said.

I agreed, saying I would continue ahead, drop my first pack, and then come back to get the rest of the gear. When I reached the end of the portage, the river was swollen to a degree I'd never seen before. I'd been in the area five years earlier during another fishing-opener weekend. The river was swift then too, but not like this. In addition, a beaver had taken down some trees near the landing, and several poplar and birch poles were stationed in the water. These trees were more or less guiding paddlers out from shore, as opposed to upriver, the way we intended to travel.

Dickes made quick work of the fallen tree over the portage. We tossed the cut logs off the trail. Within minutes, we had the rest of our gear at the top of the portage. Baxley and Kramer were just arriving at the bottom of the portage when we started our final trek up the short trail. The sun continued to shine. The canoe season was officially underway.

Dickes is an excitable, youthful human being. He's spent most of his life living in Omaha; it's his hometown, and he's proud of it. After we loaded the gear into our canoe, we stopped to put on our life jackets. Our energy was high. We felt good. After pausing for a moment, we climbed into the canoe. I guided the front of the canoe, where Dickes sat, out from shore as I got into the stern. Almost instantly, we came to a halt. A large stump sticking out just a few inches above the waterline blocked our progress.

"What way do you want to go here, Dickes?" I asked.

"Go right," he said.

We backed up the canoe no more than a foot, then proceeded forward on the right side of the stump. We took a single stroke each before the current took hold. We needed to get horizontal to the riverbank, but the bow would not turn.

"Go left," I yelled. "Dig! Dig!"

It was too late. Dickes and the front of the canoe were in the middle of the river when we capsized. When a canoe turns over, it happens in a flash. You go from sitting in the canoe to being in the water before you have a chance to process the reality of the situation. And this water, the brown, churning rapids of the Temperance River, was cold. And fast. Dickes went down the rapids first—shooting through the middle of the white water like a strange, bobbing entity traveling into an unknown darkness. I followed, desperately clutching the upside-down canoe as it barreled down the river. The current was so fast I was more than a third of the way along the fifty yards of white water on this stretch of the river within seconds. And then my torso crashed into the trunk of a dead, fallen red pine that lay in wait, hidden beneath the water's surface. The canoe immediately slid from my grasp and continued downriver. I remained, pinned to the pine.

"Help!" I yelled.

My voice seemed absent. I wondered if the impact with the tree was the reason why.

I can't hear my own voice, I remember thinking.

"Help!" I said again.

I was pinned on the log near the middle of the river. The surging river kept me locked tight against the tree while water poured over my life jacket and upper torso. My legs were under the tree. The current wanted to pull me down and under the tree, while simultaneously my top half was being nudged over the log. My body gradually took on the shape of the letter C.

"I'm pinned," I yelled, still not sure if anyone could hear me.

Dickes was now twenty yards downstream. He'd managed to get to shore, escaping from the swiftest part of the current by grabbing the overhanging branch of a cedar tree on the opposite shore.

"I don't know what was going on," Dickes later said of the situation. "I was nervous, scared, cold, wet. I look up and I see Joe pinned against the log on the right side of the rapids and water pour over [his] shoulders. And I saw his eyes. His hat was still on. His glasses were still on. His life jacket. And there was water just pouring over [his] shoulders and he wasn't moving. And I felt helpless at that moment. My friend is out there, in that freezing water temperature, stuck against the log."

Meanwhile, Baxley and Kramer did, in fact, hear my desperate screams.

"We were working on strapping in some paddles and getting things secured in the canoe so we can do the portage when all of a sudden Matthew's head kind of tilts, like he heard something. It was kind of like when a dog hears one of those dog whistles," Kramer said. "And I'm looking at Matthew like, *What do you hear?* Because I didn't hear anything. And then all of a sudden, I hear the most frantic and scared scream for help that I've ever heard [in] my life. And it still gives me goose bumps."

Baxley and Kramer dropped their gear and ran up the portage. They heard Dickes yelling from downstream, the sound now coming from below where they were. Baxley told Kramer to go check on Dickes and he would try to find me in the river.

"I heard Joe yelling from through the woods from the direction of the flowage, 'I'm pinned!'" Baxley said. "And I heard Dickes yell from downstream 'Help Joe!'"

Still caught on the tree, I quickly reasoned that nobody was going to be able to reach me. Dickes was too far downstream; it would be impossible to walk or swim upstream in the fast current. Even if he was able to make it through the trees on the opposite side of the Temperance and walk upstream, he had no chance of reaching me that far out in the river. I assumed Baxley and Kramer were unaware of the situation. I'd been in the frigid water for more than a minute at this point. I was unable to move. Something had to change, and very quickly, or I was going to die.

I reached my hands to the top of the log, where I braced myself and pushed with every ounce of strength I had, and perhaps some I didn't know I had. The force of the river was so great that it took several seconds for me to lift my body enough that my legs were no longer pinned under the tree. Eventually, I was able to essentially roll over and off the log. Only a moment before, it seemed impossible to move even an inch. Suddenly, I was free.

Unburdened by the log, I immediately started to float down the river. Momentum built quickly, as it had at the top of the rapids. Baxley came crashing through the thick alder on the bank not long after I freed myself from the log. He began to shout somewhat hysterically.

"Swim this way!" he exclaimed. "Grab a branch."

Chilled, exhausted, and confused, I did as instructed. I crawled from the shallows of the river, splashing like a dog. My thick winter boots were heavy, full of water. Our gear floated helplessly at the base of the rapids, lazily twirling about in the frothy white foam. I slowly removed my life jacket. The sun beat down on my shoulders.

Somehow, I was still alive.

Epilogue

In 2008 a firefighter in Ocala, Florida, lifted a sport utility vehicle off the ground to rescue a woman who was pinned underneath it. According to a report in the *Ocala StarBanner*, the firefighter, Chris Hickman, lifted the SUV about a foot off the pavement, allowing the other members of his squad to free an elderly woman's arm that was crushed during a rollover crash. There are other stories of individuals across the globe lifting vehicles to help someone. In another example of humans tapping into strength they didn't know they had, a mother fought a polar bear on the shore of Hudson Bay in northern Quebec in order to save her children. The woman, Lydia Angyiou, said the polar bear was "sizing up her seven-year-old," so she intervened, literally kicking and punching the seven-hundred-pound animal.

These types of scenarios involve something called "hysterical strength," and not everyone in the medical field is sold on the concept. A 2016 report by the British Broadcasting Corporation analyzes what occurs when someone is apparently able to tap into what's more commonly known as "superhuman strength." In short, it's a surge of adrenaline, motivation, and a seeming (albeit temporary) loss of pain sensitivity.

Matthew Baxley and Erik Dickes, in witnessing me get free from the fallen red pine in the Temperance River, have used the phrase "superhuman strength" to describe what they saw. Somehow I was able to untangle myself from that tree. I was pinned and could not move. Instead of waiting to see what happened, I managed to reach into the water and was able to push off. And then I was free. I don't know how it happened. It just did.

I told Rick Slatten from the St. Louis County Rescue Squad about the experience and asked him to listen to Episode 90 of the WTIP *Boundary Waters Podcast*. In the episode, one of the most listened to in the history of the podcast, Baxley, Dickes, Kevin Kramer, and I describe the sequence of events as it went down through our eyes. After Slatten listened to the episode, I shared a few more details with him about the experience. I then asked him how close I came to dying that afternoon in the Boundary Waters. In typical Slatten style, he did not mince words.

"You were a hair's breadth from dying," he said.

When I got pinned behind the fallen red pine in the river, Slatten said I became caught in what's known as a "strainer." Basically, a strainer is something that lets water but not objects flow past. In this case, I was the object. Slatten said once someone becomes bent in the letter C in a situation involving a strainer, things usually don't end well.

"That is almost impossible to overcome," he said. "And I salute your superhuman effort to push off and get yourself off the end of that log, because that single act saved your life."

Hydraulic current is incredibly powerful. I've never come up against a force so strong in my life. I did what I had to to survive. I also got lucky.

Others did not have the same twist of fate.

In the time span of about a month following our experience on the Temperance River, two people died in the BWCA. I had personal ties to both stories. The first incident involved Mike Brown, a sixty-three-year-old from Montgomery, Texas. Brown died on Seagull Lake Sunday, May 14. Cook County Search and Rescue found his body the next morning. He was wearing a life jacket.

I first met Brown in 2013 at Rockwood Lodge and Outfitters on the Gunflint Trail. Brown had been coming to the Gunflint twice every year for decades. He fished Seagull Lake in the spring and Rush Lake in the summer. He had a thick accent and was always up to talk about fishing, a topic I engaged in with him every time we met. We crossed paths only a few times over the years, but through the course of those conversations it was obvious he cared more about the Boundary Waters than almost anyone I've ever met. He died approximately forty-eight hours after I was pinned behind that pine.

The second death came about a month later, on Friday, June 23. That morning, an advanced search and rescue team, including crew members from the St. Louis County squad, found the body of eighteen-year-old Lester Hochstetler of Clear Lake, Wisconsin, on the bottom of Gillis Lake. I never met Hochstetler, but a woman named Becky at the Clear Lake Town Hall told me he was Amish, and though she'd never met him either, she understood from others in the community that he was a kind young man.

Hochstetler was not wearing his life jacket when he fell out of his canoe and into the deep waters of Gillis Lake. Hochstetler could not swim, his friends would later tell the Gunflint outfitter who rented the group their canoes. My personal connection with him is through Sean Emery, more commonly known as "Shug," who was camped on Gillis when the ordeal occurred. Shug was in the middle of an extended solo canoe trip across the Boundary Waters and was using my canoe. He posted videos of the helicopter bringing in equipment for the search and rescue mission on his YouTube channel. Shug does a bit of a play-by-play as the search operation is occurring. Literally a clown for most of his professional life, Shug is known for making people laugh, including throughout his hammock-camping videos. When he was traveling with the circus or performing at the Minnesota State Fair, Shug wasn't doing his job if people weren't having fun watching his antics. This sense of being a performer carries over to his videos in the woods or on a canoe trip. So, after a couple of minutes describing the situation wherein the young Amish man is being pulled up from the bottom of Gillis Lake, Shug switches back to being a clown. He starts having fun again. How long could he sit and dwell on the death of this stranger, after all?

I'd been working on this book for about two years by the time the summer of 2023 rolled around. Following my own near-death experience that spring, the death of Mike Brown just two days later, and Shug's experience on Gillis Lake, things were getting heavy when it came to the Boundary Waters. The region was becoming more tightly wrapped in danger and death with each passing day, it seemed. The walls of this wilderness, made of tree and stone, felt like they were closing in. Was this a dangerous place I should get away from? Everything seemed to be layered with darkness, or at least covered in a smoky, Canadian-wildfire haze. In addition, in June and July the biting insects were terrible across the Boundary Waters, and for the first time my desire to paddle a canoe or enter the wilderness started to dwindle.

Writing this book was an emotional journey. Talking with people about the death of their child, husband, brother, or dear friend is not a particularly upbeat thing to do. Complex feelings surfaced in me while I was collecting these stories. Anger, grief, sadness, denial. I felt them from others too, passed along from the stories and the people who shared them. These emotions became the bond between myself and those who lost loved ones in the Boundary Waters or nearly died themselves. However, I also felt strength and determination. Indeed, the collective strength of those who shared their stories can educate us all to travel safer and wiser through the BWCA. Those who died in the Boundary Waters and whose stories are shared in this book, they are our teachers.

Despite whatever knowledge we can glean from the deaths of Billy Cameron, Jordan Grider, Lloyd Skelton, and the others, more people will die in the Boundary Waters. Accidents will happen. Mistakes will be made. It is inevitable. However, there are things people can do to reduce their risk of dying or being seriously injured on a canoe trip to the Boundary Waters. Pay attention to the weather. Wear a life jacket. Know your limits. Use situational awareness. This is rugged country. It is not here to entertain. It is just here—a spot on the planet, however unique it might be. Sigurd Olson talks of a "singing wilderness," and sometimes that tune is merciless. Weary traveler, it does not always sing for thee.

I finished this book while at Mallard Island, the former Rainy Lake home of wilderness advocate Ernest Oberholtzer. On a rainy Friday morning, a bald eagle flew above the narrow channel separating Mallard Island and Crow Island. I saw the eagle swoop in from the west before it spread its wings and landed in a giant white pine, directly across from the Cedarbark cabin where I spent a full week in mid-August. Looking out the window, I could see and hear water splashing against the rocks. The eagle was here to pick up the remains of four walleye I had caught and cleaned the night before. It would make use of something that was now dead. This is the great cycle of things, a process by which living creatures are born, live, and die. I sat for a few moments with this understanding. Outside, the waves continued lapping on the rugged shoreline of Crow Island. The magnificent pine swayed in a steady breeze. The eagle took flight and faded from sight. It was gone. We can only guess where it would go next.

Acknowledgments

Appreciation and gratitude must be extended to those who were willing to share their stories of pain, loss, fear, and sorrow for this book to transform from memories to words on a page. Nataly Yokhanis. Ben Merry. Lisa Skelton. Members of the Grider family. And to everyone who shared their story for this book or spoke with me previously about their experiences of death and danger in the Boundary Waters, I am grateful. Many of the conversations covered difficult topics. What I learned from listening to all the people I interviewed about this general topic of death in the Boundary Waters is that the stories are actually about life— if only in the sense that life is fragile. But perhaps beyond that is the fact that we can celebrate life through death.

My job as a journalist who lives and works on the edge of the BWCA was a major factor in how this book came together. My previous reporting for WTIP Radio in Grand Marais about the Ham Lake Fire and documentaries I produced for KFAI Radio in Minneapolis both about the history of the Boundary Waters and separately about the history of fire in this region were road maps that led me to many unique and important sources of information, primarily in the form of people to talk with for this book.

Many of the interviews were conducted in Grand Marais, in Ely, or in the BWCA. Officials from the Minnesota Department of Natural Resources, members of Cook County Search and Rescue, and others accompanied me into the wilderness to show me specific locations where people had died in the BWCA. Andy McDonnell from Tuscarora Lodge and Canoe Outfitters invited me into his home to talk about the risks associated with canoe-country travel. His knowledge of the Gunflint Trail is something I will always respect.

Thanks to Rick Slatten, captain of the St. Louis County Rescue Squad, who shared countless hours with me to make sure the facts of how a search and rescue operation are performed were told the right way. Slatten spent more time talking with me than any other source. His expertise in BWCA search and rescue operations is second to none. Without Slatten, this book would be incomplete.

I wrote the bulk of this book at the Listening Point Foundation in Ely, indeed inside the home of the late Sigurd Olson, and at the Ernest Oberholtzer Foundation at Mallard Island on Rainy Lake. At Listening Point and Mallard Island I was guided by wisdom from the past, even from the mistakes of those who came before me and traveled extensively across this canoe-country wilderness. Other writing was done in a small cabin perched on the shoreline of a lake on the edge of the BWCA. This cabin belongs to Ann Possis, who has continually provided me with tremendous support during my time living in Minnesota. I can thank her for the title of this book. The rest of the manuscript I wrote inside my writer's cabin at home, not far from Lake Superior and the eastern edge of the BWCA.

My adventuring friend Matthew Baxley was willing to travel as far as necessary to help me get the stories featured in this book.

From the rolling hills of Kentucky to the far reaches of the Angleworm Trail, Baxley was there from start to finish.

Ann Ward, a delightful and kind soul, listened to me describe the people, process, and imagery involved with these stories for many hours while the book was being shaped over the course of two years.

And then there is Carley. I learned firsthand and at an early age what it means to suffer loss. Carley Spielman and I were both eighteen when she died in a car accident in Missoula, Montana, not long after we completed our first year of college at the University of Montana. Her death still stings somewhere behind my heart, in an area I never knew existed, more than twenty years later. She is the great wonder of my life.

In the coming years, others will die in the Boundary Waters. There will be more stories to share, of the dead and of those left behind. They are inevitable. These individuals will be linked to Billy Cameron. To Jordan Grider. To so many others. Their stories will be continually woven through the constructs of time. The past and the future are not unique in their assurance of pain.

And there will be many thousands of people this year, and next year, and for decades after who will complete a trip to the Boundary Waters unscathed. There will be swimming. Fishing. Sunsets that transport the mind to a better place. We must keep paddling.

About the Author

Journalist Joe Friedrichs lives on the edge of Minnesota's Boundary Waters Canoe Area Wilderness and has been reporting on the happenings in and around the region for more than a decade, sharing stories and news both in print and on public radio. This reporting has brought him to the far reaches of the BWCA, where the fishing is sublime and the stories are often raw. After graduating from the University of Montana's School of Journalism in 2005, Friedrichs worked as an environmental reporter in Oregon for eight years before moving to Minnesota. His writing has appeared in the *Star Tribune*, *Backpacker Magazine*, *Minnesota Outdoor News*, and *Lake Superior Magazine*, among many other publications. He is the author of *Her Island: The Story of Quetico's Longest Serving Interior Ranger*, and he cofounded the *Boundary Waters Podcast*, which earned the Edward R. Murrow Award in the "best podcast" category in 2020.